Dorothea Ruggles-Brise

The Musical Repository

A collection of favourite Scotch, English, and Irish songs, set to music

Dorothea Ruggles-Brise

The Musical Repository
A collection of favourite Scotch, English, and Irish songs, set to music

ISBN/EAN: 9783337411022

Printed in Europe, USA, Canada, Australia, Japan

Cover: Foto ©Thomas Meinert / pixelio.de

More available books at **www.hansebooks.com**

THE

MUSICAL

REPOSITORY:

A

COLLECTION

OF FAVOURITE

SCOTCH, ENGLISH, AND IRISH

SONGS,

SET TO MUSIC.

GLASGOW:

PRINTED BY ALEX. ADAM,

FOR A. CARRICK, BOOKSELLER, SALTMARKET,

1799.

CONTENTS.

CONTENTS.

CONTENTS.

CONTENTS.

THE

MUSICAL

REPOSITORY:

A COLLECTION OF

SONGS,

SET TO MUSIC.

B

MUSICAL REPOSITORY.

SONG I.

THE WOUNDED HUSSAR.

Moderate.

A-lone to the banks of the dark roll - ing

Danube, Fair A - de - laid hied when the battle

was o'er; O whi - ther, fhe cried, haft thou

wan - der'd, my lov - er, Or here doft thou

welter and bleed on the shore? What

voice did I hear! 'twas my Henry that sigh'd, All

mournful she hasten'd, nor wander'd a-far, When

bleeding a-lone on the heath she def-cried,

By the light of the moon, her poor

wound - ed hussar.

From his bofom that heav'd, the laft torrent was ftreaming,
And pale was his vifage, deep mark'd with a fcar,
And dim was that eye, once expreffively beaming,
That melted in love, and that kindled in war;
How fmit was poor Adelaid's heart at the fight!
How bitter fhe wept o'er the victim of war!
" Haft thou come, my fond love, this laft forrowful night,
To cheer the lone heart of your wounded huffar."

" Thou fhalt live!" fhe replied, " heaven's mercy relieving,
Each anguifhing wound fhall forbid me to mourn;"
" Ah! no, the laft pang in my bofom is heaving,
No light of the morn fhall to Henry return;
Thou charmer of life, ever tender and true,
Ye babes of my love, that await me afar—"
His falt'ring tongue fcarcely murmur'd adieu,
When he funk in her arms, the poor wounded huffar.

SONG II.

To the foregoing Tune.

BE hufh'd the loud breeze, and foft roll the rough billow
That curls its rude head o'er my fweet Billy's grave;
No peace ere fhall gladden the heart of his Anna,
Her hope is entombed in the Texel's proud wave.
On the coaft of Mynheer, with his broad pendant flying,
Tho' Duncan his enfign of triumph could rear,
Britannia fhall weep when her warriors are dying,
And the eyes of her fair be bedew'd with a tear.

No more my fond bofom, with rapture reclining,
My Billy fhall tell of the laurels he won;
How midft the wide carnage he thought of his Anna,
And ne'er was the man that would flinch from his gun.
No danger he fear'd when the foe was affailing,
Nor minded the ftorm, nor the cannon's loud roar,
In hopes foon at home to be moor'd with his Anna,
And figh in her arms when the battle was o'er.

The day dawns with joy when the heart feels no forrow,
But heart-foothing fleep flies the pillow of care,
On the hopelefs eye dawns no happy to-morrow,
It rifes in fadnefs to fet in defpair.
Yet a few other funs, and the conflict is over,
This poor aching trembler to beat will give o'er,
In the cold arms of death I'll reft with my lover,
When the fate of the battle fhall part us no more.

SONG III.

THE MAID THAT TENDS THE GOATS.

Slow.

Up amang yon cliffy rocks, Sweetly rings the

rifing e-cho, To the maid that tends the goats,

Lilting o'er her native notes. Hark! fhe fings,

" Young Sandy's kind, An' he's promis'd ay to

lo'e me; Here's a brotch I ne'er fhall tine

Till he's fairly marry'd to me. Drive away, ye

drone, Time, An' bring about our bridal day.

" Sandy herds a flock o' fheep,
" Aften does he blaw the whiftle,
" In a ftrain fae faftly fweet,
" Lammies, lift'ning, dare nae bleat.
" He's as fleet's the mountain roe,
" Hardy as the Highland heather,
" Wading thro' the winter fnow,
" Keeping ay his flock together,
" But a plaid, wi' bare houghs,
" He braves the bleakeft norlin blaft.

" Brawly he can dance and fing,
" Canty glee or Highland cronach;
" Nane can ever match his fling
" At a reel, or round a ring.
" Wightly can he wield a rung;
" In a brawl he's ay the bangfter;
" A' his praife can ne'er be fung
" By the langeft winded fangfter,
" Sangs that fing o' Sandy
" Come fhort, tho' they were e'er fae lang."

SONG IV.

THOU SOFT FLOWING AVON.

Largetto.

Thou foft flowing Avon, by thy filver

ftream, Of things more than mor-tal thy

Shakefpeare would dream, would dream, would

dream, thy Shakefpeare would dream. The

fairies, by moon-light, dance round his

green bed; For hallow'd the turf is which

pil-low'd his head: The fairies, by moon-

light, dance round his green bed; For hal-

low'd the turf is which   pil - low'd his head.

The love-ſtricken maiden, the ſoft ſighing ſwain,
Here rove without danger, and ſigh without pain.
The ſweet bud of beauty no blight ſhall here dread;
For hallow'd the turf is which pillow'd his head.

Here youth ſhall be fam'd for their love and their truth;
And cheerful old age feel the ſpirit of youth,
For the raptures of fancy here poets ſhall tread;
For hallow'd the turf is which pillow'd his head.

Flow on, ſilver Avon, in ſong ever flow!
Be the ſwans on thy borders ſtill whiter than ſnow!
Ever full be thy ſtream; like his fame may it ſpread!
And the turf ever hallow'd which pillow'd his head!

C

SONG V.

THE SNUG LITTLE ISLAND.

Allegretto.

Daddy Neptune one day to Freedom did

say, If e-ver I liv'd upon dry land, The

fpot I fhou'd hit on would be little Britain, Says

Free-dom, Why that's my own ifl-and.

Oh! what a fnug lit-tle ifl-and, A

right lit - tle tight lit - tle ifl - and;

All the globe round, none can be found So

happy as this lit - tle ifland.

Julius Cefar the Roman, who yielded to no man,
   Came by water, he couldn't come by land;
And Dane, Pict, and Saxon their homes turn'd their backs on,
   And all for the fake of our ifland.
     Oh what a fnug little ifland,
      They'd all have a touch at the ifland;
   Some were fhot dead,—fome of them fled,
     And fome ftaid to live in the ifland.

Then a very great war-man, call'd Billy the Norman,
   Cried, D—n it, I never liked my land,
It wou'd be much more handy to leave this Normandy;
   And live on yon beautiful ifland.
     Says he, 'Tis a fnug little ifland,
      Shan't us go vifit the ifland;
   Hop, fkip, and jump,—there he was plump,
     And he kick'd up a duft in the ifland.

Yet party deceit help'd the Normans to beat,
  Of traitors they managed to buy land;
By Dane, Saxon, or Pict we ne'er had been lick'd,
  Had they stuck to the king of the island.
    Poor Harold the king of the island,
    He lost both his life and his island;
    That's very true,—what could he do?
    Like a Briton he died for the island.

Then the Spanish Armada set out to invade a,
  Quite sure, if they ever came nigh land,
They cou'dn't do less than tuck up Queen Bess,
  And take their full swing in the island.
    Oh the poor queen and the island,
    The drones came to plunder the island;
    But snug in her hive—the queen was alive,
    And buz was the word at the island.

The proud puff'd up cakes thought to make ducks and drakes
  Of our wealth, but they scarcely could spy land,
E'er Drake had the luck to make their pride duck,
  And stoop to the lads of the island.
    Huzza! for the lads of the island,
    The good wooden walls of the island;
    Devil or Don,—let 'em come on,
    But how would they come off at the island?

I don't wonder much that the French and the Dutch
  Have since been oft tempted to try land,
And I wonder much less they have met no success,
  For why should we give up our island?

Oh 'tis a wonderful ifland!
All of 'em long for the ifland;
Hold a bit there, (let 'em)—take fire and air,
But we'll have the fea and the ifland.

Then fince Freedom and Neptune have hitherto kept tune,
In each faying, This fhall be my land,
Shou'd the army of England, or all they cou'd bring, land,
We'd fhow 'em fome play for the ifland;
We'd fight for our right to the ifland,
We'd give 'em enough of the ifland;
Frenchmen fhou'd juft—bite at our duft,
But not a bit more of the ifland.

SONG VI.

HEARTS OF OAK.

Allegro Moderato.

Come cheer up my lads, 'tis to glory we fteer, To

add fomething more to this wonderful year; To

honour we call you, not prefs you like flaves, For

who are fo free as we fons of the waves. Hearts of

oak are our fhips, hearts of oak are our men, We

al‐ways are ready, Steady, boys, steady, We'll

fight and we'll conquer a‐gain and again.

We ne'er see our foes but we wish them to stay,
They never see us but they wish us away,
If they run, why we follow, and run them ashore,
For if they won't fight us we cannot do more.
Hearts of oak, &c.

They swear they'll invade us these terrible foes,
They frighten our women, our children, and beaux,
But shou'd their flat bottoms in darkness get o'er,
Still Britons they'll find to receive them on shore.
Hearts of oak, &c.

We'll still make 'em run, and we'll still make 'em sweat,
In spite of the devil and Brussels Gazette;
Then cheer up my lads, with one heart let us sing,
Our soldiers, our sailors, our statesmen, and king.
Hearts of oak, &c.

SONG VII.

ON ADMIRAL DUNCAN'S VICTORY.

Enroll'd in our bright annals lives full

many a gallant name, But never British

heart conceiv'd a prouder deed of fame, But

never British heart con-ceiv'd, But never

British heart con-ceiv'd a prouder deed of

fame, A prouder deed of fame. To shield our

li - ber - ties and laws, to guard our sov'reign's

crown, Than noble Duncan's mighty arm at-

chiev'd off Camperdown. To shield our liber-

ties and laws, to guard our sov'reign's crown, Im-

mortal be the glorious deed at - chiev'd off

Cam - per - down.

D

October the eleventh it was, he fpied the Dutch at nine,
The Britifh fignal flew to break their clofe embattled line ;
Their line was broke, for all our tars, on that aufpicious day,
All bitter memory of the paft had vowed to wipe away.

Their line was broke, &c.

At three o'clock nine mighty fhips had ftruck their colours
    proud,
And two brave admirals at his feet their vanquifh'd flags had
    bow'd;
Our Duncan's towering colours ftream'd all honour to the laft,
For, in the battle's fierceft rage, he nail'd them to the maft.

Our Duncan's towering colours, &c.

The victory was now complete ; the cannon ceas'd to roar;
The fcatter'd remnants of the foe flunk to their native fhore ;
No power the pride of conqueft had his heart to lead aftray,
He fummon'd his triumphant crew, and this was heard to fay:

CHORUS.

" Let every man now bend the knee, and here in folemn pray'r,
" Give thanks to God, who in this fight has made our caufe
    his care."

Then on the deck, the noble field of that proud day's renown,
Brave Duncan with his crew devout before their God knelt
    down,
And humbly blefs'd his Providence, and hail'd his guardian
    power,
Who valour, ftrength, and fkill infpir'd in that dread battle's
    hour.

And humbly blefs'd, &c.

'The captive Dutch this folemn fcene furvey'd with filent awe,
And rue'd the day when Holland join'd to France's impious
   law,
And marked how virtue, courage, faith, unite to form this
   land,
For victory, for fame and power, juft rule, and high command,
     And marked, &c.

The Venerable was the fhip that bore his flag to fame,
Our veteran hero well becomes his gallant veffel's name;
Behold his locks! they fpeak the toil of many a ftormy day;
For fifty years and more, my boys, has fighting been his way.

GRAND CHORUS.

Behold his locks! they fpeak the toil of many a ftormy day,
For fifty years and more, my boys, has fighting been his way;
The Venerable was the fhip that bore his flag to fame,
And venerable ever be our vet'ran Duncan's name!

SONG VIII.

THE BIRKS OF INVERMAY.

The smiling morn, the breath - ing spring,

In - - vite the tuneful birds to sing, And

while they warble from each spray, Love

melts the u - - ni - - ver - - fal lay. Let

us, A - - man - - da, time - - - ly wise, Like

them improve the hour that flies, And

in foft raptures wafte the day, a - - mong

the birks of In - - ver - may.

For foon the winter of the year,
And age, life's winter, will appear,
At this thy living bloom will fade,
As that will ftrip thy verdant fhade;
Our tafte of pleafure then is o'er,
The feather'd fongfters are no more;
And when they droop, and we decay,
Adieu the birks of Invermay.

Behold the hills and vales around,
With lowing herds and flocks abound;
The wanton kids and frifking lambs,
Gambol and dance about their dams;
The bufy bees with humming noife,
And all the reptile kind rejoice;
Let us, like them, then fing and play
About the birks of Invermay.

Hark, how the waters as they fall,
Loudly my love to gladneſs call:
The wanton waves ſport in the beams,
And fiſhes play throughout the ſtreams;
The circling ſun does now advance,
And all the planets round him dance:
Let us as jovial be as they
Among the birks of Invermay.

SONG IX.

THE VICAR AND MOSES.

At the ſign of the horſe, old Spintext

of courſe, Each night took his pipe and his

pot, O'er a jorum of nap--py, quite

pleafant and happy, Was plac'd this ca-no-

nical fot, Tol de rol de rol ti

dol di dol.

The evening was dark, when in came the clerk,
  With reverence due and fubmiffion;
Firft ftrok'd his cravat, then twirl'd round his hat,
  And bowing, preferr'd his petition.

I'm come, Sir, faid he, to beg, look d'ye fee,
  Of your reverend werfhip and glory,
To inter a poor baby, with as much fpeed as may be,
  And I'll walk with the lanthorn before you.

The body we'll bury, but pray where's the hurry?
  Why Lord, Sir, the corpfe it does ftay:
You fool hold your peace, fince miracles ceafe,
  A corpfe, Mofes, can't run away.

Then Mofes he fmil'd, faying, Sir, a fmall child
  Cannot long delay your intentions

Why that's true, by St. Paul, a child that is fmall
    Can never enlarge its dimenfions.

Bring Mofes fome beer, and bring me fome, d'ye hear,
    I hate to be call'd from my liquor:
Come, Mofes, the King, 'tis a fcandalous thing,
    Such a fubject fhould be but a Vicar.

Then Mofes he fpoke, Sir, 'tis paft twelve o'clock,
    Befides there's a terrible fhower;
Why Mofes, you elf, fince the clock has ftruck twelve,
    I'm fure it can never ftrike more.

Befides, my dear friend, this leffon attend,
    Which to fay and to fwear I'll be bold,
That the corpfe, fnow or rain, can't endanger, that's plain,
    But perhaps you or I may take cold.

Then Mofes went on, Sir the clock has ftruck one,
    Pray mafter look up at the hand;
Why it ne'er can ftrike lefs, 'tis a folly to prefs
    A man for to go that can't ftand.

At length hat and cloak old Orthodox took,
    But cram'd his jaw with a quid;
Each tipt off a gill for fear they fhould chill,
    And then ftagger'd away fide by fide.

When come to the grave, the clerk hum'd a ftave,
    Whilft the furplice was wrapt round the prieft;
Where fo droll was the figure of Mofes and Vicar,
    That the parifh ftill talk of the jeft.

Good people, let's pray, put the corpfe t'other way,
   Or perchance I will over it ftumble;
'Tis beft to take care, tho' the fages declare,
   A *mortuum caput* can't tremble.

Woman that's born of a man, that's wrong, the leaf's torn:
   A man, that is born of a woman,
Can't continue an hour, but's cut down like a flow'r;
   You fee, Mofes, death fpareth no man.

Here Mofes do look, what a confounded book;
   Sure the letters are turn'd upfide down,
Such a fcandalous print! fure the devil is in't,
   That this Bafket fhould print for the Crown.

Prithee, Mofes, you read, for I cannot proceed,
   And bury the corpfe in my ftead.
        (Amen, Amen.)
Why, Mofes, you're wrong, pray hold ftill your tongue,
   You've taken the tail for the head.

O where's thy fting, Death! put the corpfe in the earth,
   For, believe me, 'tis terrible weather:
So the corpfe was interr'd, without praying a word,
   And away they both ftagger'd together,
      Singing 'Tol de rol ti dol di dol.

E

SONG X.

THE SAILOR'S CONSOLATION.

Andantino.

Spanking Jack was fo comely, fo pleafant, fo

jolly, 'Tho' winds blew great guns, ftill he'd whiftle

and fing, Jack lov'd his friend, and was true to

his Molly, And if honour gives greatnefs, was

great as a king. One night as we drove with two

reefs in   the   mainfail, And the fcud came on

low'r - ing up - on a lee fhore, Jack went up

a - loft for to hand the top gal'nt - fail, A

fpray wafh'd him off, and we ne'er faw him more, We

ne'er faw him more. But grieving's a folly, come

let us be jolly, If we've troubles at fea

boys, we've pleafures afhore.

E 2

Whiffling Tom ſtill of miſchief or fun in the middle,
　　Through life in all weathers at random would jog,
He'd dance and he'd ſing, and he'd play on the fiddle,
　　And ſwig with an air his allowance of grog:
Long ſide of a Don in the Terrible frigate,
　　As yard arm and yard arm we lay off the ſhore,
In and out whiffling Tom did ſo caper and jig it,
　　That his head was ſhot off, and we ne'er ſaw him more!
　　　　But grieving's a folly, &c.

Bonny Ben was to each jolly meſsmate a brother,
　　He was manly and honeſt, good natur'd and free,
If ever one tar was more true than another,
　　To his friend and his duty, that ſailor was he:
One day with the davit to heave the cadge anchor,
　　Ben went in the boat on a bold craggy ſhore,
He overboard tipt, when a ſhark and a ſpanker
　　Soon nipt him in two, and we ne'er ſaw him more!
　　　　But grieving's a folly, &c.

But what of it all lads? ſhall we be down hearted,
　　Becauſe that mayhap we now take our laſt ſup?
Life's cable muſt one day or other be parted,
　　And death in faſt mooring will bring us all up.
But 'tis always the way on't; one ſcarce finds a brother,
　　Fond as pitch, honeſt, hearty, and true to the core,
But by battle or ſtorm, or ſome d—n'd thing or other,
　　He's popp'd off the hooks, and we ne'er ſee him more.
　　　　But grieving's a folly, &c.

SONG XI.

JENNY'S BAWBEE.

Moderato.

I met four chaps yon birks amang, Wi'

hanging lugs and faces lang, I speer'd at

niebour Bauldy Strang, What are they these we see?

Quoth he, " Ilk cream-fac'd pawky chiel, Thinks

himsell cunning as the deil, And here they

cam' awa' to steal, Jenny's bawbee."

The firſt, a captain to his trade,
Wi' ill-lin'd ſcull, and back weel clad,
March'd roun' the barn and by the ſhed,
     And papped on his knee;
Quoth he, " My goddeſs, nymph, and queen,
" Your beauty's dazzl'd baith my een;"
But deil a beauty he had ſeen,
    But Jenny's bawbee.

A norlan' laird neiſt trotted up,
Wi' baſſen'd nag and ſiller whup,
Cry'd, " Here's my beaſt, lad had the grup,
     " Or tie him to a tree:
" What's goud to me ? I've wealth o' lan',
" Beſtow on ane o' worth your han';"
He thought to pay what he was awn,
    Wi' Jenny's bawbee.

A lawyer neiſt, wi' blatherin' gab,
Wi' ſpeeches wove like ony wab,
In ilk anes corn he took a dab,
     And a' for a fee;
Accounts he owed thro' a the town,
And tradeſmens tongues nae mair cou'd drown,
But now he thought to clout his gown,
    Wi' Jenny's bawbee.

Quite ſpruce, juſt frae the waſhing tubs,
A fool came neiſt, but life has rubs,
Foul were the roads, and fu' the dubs,
     And fair beſmear'd was he;
He danc'd up, ſquintin' thro' a glaſs,
And grinn'd, " I' faith a bonny laſs,"
He thought to win, wi' front of braſs,
    Jenny's bawbee.

She bad the laird gae kaim his wig,
The foger not to ftrut fae big,
The lawyer not to be a prig,
   The fool he cried, " Tee-hee,
" I ken'd that I could never fail,"
But fhe prinn'd the difh-clout to his tail,
And cool'd him wi' a water-pail,
   And kept her bawbee.

Then Johnny cam', a lad o' fenfe,
Altho' he had na mony pence,
He took young Jenny to the fpence,
   Wi' her to crack a wee;
Now Johnny was a clever chiel,
And here his fuit he prefs'd fae weel,
That Jenny's heart grew faft as jeel,
   And fhe birl'd her bawbee.

SONG XII.

CRAZY JANE.

[The following was written in confequence of a Lady having in her walks, during a refidence in the country, met a poor mad woman, known by the above appellation, at whofe appearance the Lady was much alarmed.]

Tune—*Gin ye meet a bonny laffie.*

Why, fair maid, in ev'-ry feature, Are such

figns of fear exprefs'd? Can a wand'ring, wretch-

ed creature, With fuch terror fill thy breaft?

Do my frenzied looks a - - larm thee? Truft me,

fweet, thy fears are vain; Not for kingdoms would

I harm thee; Shun not then poor

cra - zy Jane.

Doft thou weep to fee my anguifh?
  Mark me, and avoid my woe;
When men flatter, figh, and languifh,
  Think them falfe—I found them fo.
For I lov'd, oh fo fincerely!
  None could ever love again!
But the youth I lov'd fo dearly,
  Stole the wits of crazy Jane.

Fondly my young heart receiv'd him,
  Which was doom'd to love but one;
He figh'd—he vow'd—and I believ'd him,
  He was falfe, and I undone.
From that hour, has reafon never
  Held her empire o'er my brain;
Henry fled—with him for ever
  Fled the wits of crazy Jane.

Now forlorn and broken hearted,
  And with frenzied thoughts befet,
On that fpot where once we parted,
  On that fpot where firft me met,
Still I fing my love-lorn ditty,
  Still I flowly pace the plain;
Whilft each paffer-by, in pity,
  Cries, " God help thee, crazy Jane."
              F

SONG XIII.

THE COTTAGE ON THE MOOR.

My mam is no more, and my dad in his

grave, Little or - phans are fiſ - - ter and

I, ſad - - ly poor; In - - - duſ - try our wealth,

and no dwell - - ing we have, But yon

neat li.tle cot - - tage that ſt nds on the

moor. Yon neat lit - tle cot - tage, Yon

neat lit - - tle cottage, Yon neat lit - tle

cot - tage that ftands on the moor.

The lark's early fong does to labour invite;
   Contented, we juft keep the wolf from the door;
And, Phœbus retiring, trip home with delight,
   To our neat little cottage that ftands on the moor.
      Yon neat little cottage, &c.

Our meals are but homely, mirth fweetens our cheer,
   Affection's our inmate, the gueft we adore;
And heart-eafe and health make a palace appear
   Of our neat little cottage that ftands on the moor.
      Yon neat little cottage, &c.

F 2.

SONG XIV.

CELEBRATED DEATH-SONG OF THE CHEROKEE INDIAN.

The sun sets at night, and the stars shun the day, But glory remains when their lights fade a - - - - - way: Begin, ye tormentors, your threats are in vain, For the son of Alk - - no - - mook shall ne - - - - ver

com - - plain;   For   the   fon   of   Alknomook

will   ne - ver   complain.

Remember the arrows he fhot from his bow,
Remember your chiefs by his hatchet laid low;
Why fo flow?—Do you wait till I fhrink from the pain?
No!—the fon of Alknomook fhall never complain.
            No!—the fon, &c.

Remember the wood where in ambufh we lay,
And the fcalps which we bore from your nation away.
Now the flame rifes faft, they exult in my pain;
But the fon of Alknomook can never complain.
            But the fon, &c.

I go to the land where my father is gone;
His ghoft fhall rejoice in the fame of his fon.
Death comes as a friend, he relieves me from pain;
And the fon of Alknomook has fcorn'd to complain!
            And the fon, &c.

SONG XV.

ROSLIN CASTLE.

'Twas in that fea-fon of the year,

When all things gay and fweet appear, That

Co-lin, with the morn - - - ing ray, A-
ir.

rofe and fung his ru-ral lay. Of

Nanny's charms the fhep-herd fung, The

hills and dales with Nan - - - - ny rung, While

Rof - - lin caftle heard the fwain, And
e - - cho'd back the cheerful ftrain.

Awake, fweet mufe! the breathing fpring
With rapture warms; awake and fing!
Awake and join the vocal throng
Who hail the morning with a fong!
To Nanny raife the cheerful lay;
O bid her hafte and come away;
In fweeteft fmiles herfelf adorn,
And add new graces to the morn.

O hark, my love! on ev'ry fpray
Each feather'd warbler tunes his lay!
'Tis beauty fires the ravifh'd fong,
And love infpires the melting throng.
Then let my raptur'd notes arife:
For beauty darts from Nanny's eyes;
And love my rifing bofom warms,
And fills my foul with fweet alarms.

O come, my love! thy Colin's lay
With rapture calls; O come away!
Come, while the mufe this wreath fhall twine
Around that modeft brow of thine!
O hither hafte, and with thee bring
That beauty blooming like the fpring
Thofe graces that divinely fhine!
And charm this ravifh'd breaft of mine.

SONG XVI.

To the foregoing Tune.

FROM Roflin Caftle's echoing walls
Refounds my fhepherd's ardent calls;
My Colin bids me come away,
And love demands I fhould obey.
His melting ftrain and tuneful lay
So much the charms of love difplay,
I yield,—nor longer can refrain
To own my love, and blefs my fwain.

No longer can my heart conceal
The painful pleafing flame I feel;
My foul retorts the am'rous ftrain,
And echoes back in love again.
Where lurks my fongfter? From what grove
Does Colin pour his notes of love?
O bring me to the happy bow'r
Where mutual love may blifs fecure.

Ye vocal hills that catch the fong,
Repeating, as it flies along,
To Colin's ear my ftrain convey,
And fay, I hafte to come away.
Ye zephyrs foft that fan the gale,
Waft to my love the foothing tale;
In whifpers all my foul exprefs,
And tell, I hafte his arms to blefs.

SONG XVII.

DONNEL AND FLORA.

When mer - ry hearts were gay, Carelefs of

ought but play, Poor Flo - - ra flipt a - way,

Sad'ning to Mo - ra: Loofe flow'd her coal-

black hair, Quick heav'd her befom bare, And

thus to the troubled air, She vented her

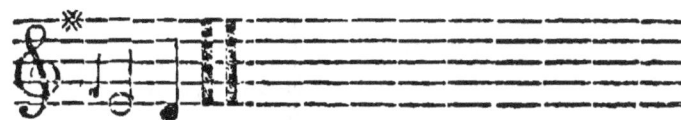

forrow.

" Loud howls the northern blaſt,
" Bleak is the dreary waſte ;—
" Haſte then, **O Donnel** haſte,
　　" Haſte to thy Flora.
" Twice twelve long months are o'er,
" Since in a foreign ſhore
" You promis'd to fight no more,
　　" But meet me in Mora.

" Where now is Donnel dear ?"
. " Maids cry with taunting ſneer,
" Say, is he ſtill ſincere
　　" To his lov'd Flora ?"
" Parents upbraid my moan,
" Each heart is turn'd to ſtone—
" Ah, Flora! thou'rt now alone,
　　" Friendleſs in Mora !

" Come then, O come away,
" Donnel no longer ſtay ;
" Where can my rover ſtray
　　" From his dear Flora ?
" Ah ſure he ne'er could be
" Falſe to his vows to me—
" O heaven ! is not yonder he
　　" Bounding in Mora ?"

" Never, O wretched fair,
{Sigh'd the ſad meſſenger)
" Never ſhall Donnel mair
　　" Meet his lov'd Flora.
" Cold, cold, beyond the main,
" Donnel thy love lies ſlain ;
" He ſent me to ſoothe thy pain,
　　" Weeping in Mora.

" Well fought our gallant men,
" Headed by brave Burgoyne;
" Our heroes were thrice led on
  " To Britiſh glory:
" But ah! tho' our foes did flee,
" Sad was the loſs to thee, '
" While every freſh victory
  " Drown'd us in ſorrow."

" Here, take this truſty blade,"
(Donnel expiring, ſaid)
" Give it to yon dear maid
  " Weeping in Mora.
" Tell her, O Allan, tell,
" Donnel thus bravely fell,
" And that in his laſt farewell,
  !" He thought on his Flora."

Mute ſtood the trembling fair,
Speechleſs with wild deſpair,
Then ſtriking her boſom bare,
  Sigh'd out, " Poor Flora!
" Oh Donnel! Oh welladay!"
Was all the fond heart could ſay;
At length the ſound died away,
  Feebly in Mora.

SONG XVIII.

SWEET LILLIES OF THE VALLEY.

O'er barren hills and flow'ry dales, O'er

feas and diftant fhores, With mer - ry fong

and jo - cund tales, I've pafs'd fome pleafant

hours.   Though wand' - ring thus, I

ne'er could find A girl like blith'fome

Sally, Who picks and culls, and cries a-

loud, Who picks and culls, and cries aloud,

Sweet lil--lies of the valley, Sweet

lil--lies of the valley; Who picks and

culls, and cries aloud, Sweet lil-lies of the

val-ley.

From whiftling o'er the harrow'd turf,
    From nefting of each tree,
I chofe a foldier's life to lead,
    So focial, gay, and free :
Yet tho' the laffes love as well,
    And often try to rally,
None pleafes me like her that cries,
    Sweet lillies of the valley.

I'm now return'd (of late difcharg'd)
    To ufe my native toil,
From fighting in my country's caufe,
    To plough my country's foil ;
I care not which, with either pleas'd,
    So I poffefs my Sally,
That little merry nymph that cries,
    Sweet lillies of the valley.

ask'd 'bout all he faw, 'Twas Monfieur Je vous

n'entend pas.

John to the Palais Royal come,
Its fplendour almoft ftruck him dumb;
I fay, whofe houfe is that there here?
Hoffe! Je vous n'entends pas Monfieur.
What Nong Tong Paw again? cries John,
This fellow is fome mighty Don!
No doubt h'as plenty for the maw,
I'll breakfaft with this Nong Tong Paw.

John faw Verfailles from Marli's height,
And cried, aftonifh'd at the fight,
Whofe fine eftate is that there here?
Stat! Je vous n'entends pas Monfieur.
His? what the land and houfes too?
The fellow's richer than a Jew!
On every thing he lays his claw,
I fhould like to dine with Nong Tong Paw.

Next tripping came a courtly fair;
John cried, enchanted with her air,
What lovely wench is that there here?
Ventch! Je vous n'entends pas Monfieur.
What, he again? upon my life;
A palace, lands, and then a wife;
Sir Jofhua might delight to draw;
I fhould like to fup with Nong Tong Paw.

But hold, whofe funeral's that? cries John:
je vous n'entends pas: what! is he gone?
Wealth, fame, and beauty could not fave
Poor Nong 'Tong Paw then from the grave:
His race is run, his game is up,
I'd with him breakfaft, dine, and fup,
But fince he chufes to withdraw,
Good-night t'ye Mounfeer Nong Tong Paw.

SONG XXI.

LASH'D TO THE HELM,

Andantino.

In ftorms, when clouds obfcure the fky, And
thun-ders roll and light-nings fly, In midft
of all thefe dire alarms, I think, my Sal-ly,
on thy charms, The troubled main, The wind

and rain, My ar--dent paſ--ſion prove

Laſh'd to the helm, Shou'd ſeas o'erwhelm, I'd

think on thee, my love, I'd think on thee,

my love, I'd think on thee, my love

Laſh'd to the helm, Shou'd ſeas o'erwhelm, I'd

think on thee my love.

When rocks appear on ev'ry fide,
And art is vain the fhip to guide,
In varied fhapes when death appears,
The thoughts of thee my bofom cheers:
     The troubled main,
     The wind and rain,
My ardent paffion prove;
     Lafh'd to the helm,
     Shou'd feas o'erwhelm,
I'd think on thee my love.

But fhou'd the gracious pow'rs be kind,
Difpel the gloom and ftill the wind,
And waft me to thy arms once more,
Safe to my long-loft native fhore;
     No more the main
     I'd tempt again,
But tender joys improve;
     I then with thee
     Shou'd happy be,
And think on nought but love.

SONG XXII.

THE SAILOR'S JOURNAL.

Andantino.

'Twas poſt me---ri---dian, half paſt four,

By ſig--nal I from Nancy parted; At ſix

ſhe lin---ger'd on the ſhore, With uplift

hands and broken hearted: At ſev'n, while taught'-

ning the fore-ſtay, I ſaw her faint, or elſe

'twas fancy; At eight we all got under weigh,

And bid a long adieu to Nancy.

'Twas night, and now eight bells had rung,
　　When carelefs faïlors ever cheery,
On the mid-watch fo cheerful fung,
　　With tempers labours cannot weary.
I, little to their mirth inclin'd,
　　For tender wifhes fill'd my fancy,
And my warm fighs increas'd the wind,
　　Look'd on the moon, and thought on Nancy.

And now arriv'd that jovial night,
　　When ev'ry true bred tar caroufes,
Around the grog all hands delight,
　　To toaft their fweethearts and their fpoufes.
Round went the fong, the jeft, the glee,
　　And youthful thoughts fill every fancy,
And when in turn it came to me,
　　I heav'd a figh, and toafted Nancy.

Next morn a ftorm came on at four;
　　At fix the elements in motion,
Plung'd me, and three poor failors more,
　　Headlong into the foaming ocean;

Poor wretches, they foon found their graves,
    For me it may be only fancy,
But love feem'd to forbid the waves
    To fnatch me from the arms of Nancy.

Scarce the foul hurricane was clear'd,
    Scarce winds and waves had ceas'd to rattle,
When a bold enemy appear'd,
    And dauntlefs we prepar'd for battle.
And now, while fome lov'd friend or wife
    Like lightning rufh'd on every fancy,
To Providence I trufted life,
    Put up a pray'r, and thought on Nancy,

At laft, 'twas in the month of May,
    The crew, it being lovely weather,
At three, A. M. difcover'd day,
    And England's chalky cliffs together:
At feven, up channel how we bore!
    While hopes and fears rufh'd on my fancy;
At twelve, I gaily jump'd afhore,
    And to my throbbing heart prefs'd Nancy.

SONG XXIII.

SAVOURNA DELISH.

Oh! the moment was sad when my love and

I   parted,   Sa - vour -- na   De -- lish

Shighan Oh! As I kifs'd off her tears, I   was

nigh broken   hearted,   Sa --- vour - na   De-

lifh   Shighan   Oh!   Wan was her cheek which

hung on my ſhoulder, Damp was her hand, no

marble was colder, I felt that I never

a-gain ſhould be-hold her; Sa-vour--na

De--liſh Shighan Oh.

When the word of command put our men into motion,
  Savourna, &c.
I buckl'd my knapſack to croſs the wide ocean,
  Savourna, &c.
Briſk were our troops, all rearing like thunder,
Pleas'd with the voyage, impatient for plunder,
My boſom with grief was almoſt torn aſundɤr.
  Savourna, &c.

I 2

Long I fought for my country, far, far from my true love,
        Savourna, &c.
All my pay and my booty I hoarded for you love,
        Savourna, &c.
Peace was proclaim'd; efcap'd from the flaughter,
Landed at home, my fweet girl, I fought her,
But forrow, alas! to her cold grave had brought her.
        Savourna, &c.

SONG XXIV.

JOHN ANDERSON, MY JOE.

john Anderfon my joe, John, when we were

firft acquaint, Your locks were like the raven, your

bonny brow was brent; But now you're turned

bald, John, your locks are like the fnow, Yet

bleffings on your frofty pow, John Anderfon

my joe.

John Anderfon my joe, John, ye were my firft conceit,
And ay at kirk and market I've kept you trim and neat;
There's fome folk fay your failing, John, but I fcarce believe
    it's fo,
For you're ay the fame kind man to me, John Anderfon
    my joe.

John Anderfon my joe, John, we've feen our bairns' bairns,
And yet, my dear John Anderfon, I'm happy in your arms,
And fae are ye in mine, John, I'm fure ye'll ne'er fay no,
Tho' the days are gane that we hae feen, John Anderfon
    my joe.

John Anderfon my joe, John, our filler ne'er was rife,
And yet we ne'er faw poverty fin' we were man and wife;
We've ay haen bit and brat, John, great bleffings here below,
And that helps to keep peace at hame, John Anderfon my joe.

John Anderfon my joe, John, the warld lo'es us baith,
We ne'er fpake ill o' neighbours, John, nor did them ony
        fkaith,
To live in peace and quietnefs was a' our care, ye know,
And I'm fure they'll greet when we are dead, John Anderfon
        my joe.

John Anderfon my joe, John, frae year to year we've paft,
And foon that year maun come, John, will bring us to our
        laft;
But let na' that affright us, John, our hearts were ne'er our
        foe,
While in innocent delight we liv'd, John Anderfon, my joe.

John Anderfon my joe, John, we clamb the hill thegither,
And mony a canty day, John, we've had wi' ane anither;
Now we maun totter down, John, but hand in hand we'll
        go,
And we'll fleep thegither at the foot, John Anderfon my joe.

SONG XXV.

HOW SWEET IN THE WOODLANDS.

Moderato.

How sweet in the wood - lands, with

fleet hounds and horn, To waken shrill

e - cho, and taste the fresh morn;

But hard is the chace my fond heart must

pur - - sue, For Daph - ne, fair Daph - - ne,

is loſt to my view ; She's loſt, Fair

Daphne is loſt to my view.

Aſſiſt me, chaſte Dian, the nymph to regain,
More wild than the roe-buck, and wing'd with diſdain;
In pity o'ertake her, who wounds as ſhe flies,
Tho' Daphne's purſu'd, 'tis Myrtillo that dies,—
                        That dies!
    Tho' Daphne's purſu'd, &c.

SONG XXVI.

LEANDER ON THE BAY.

Le - - ander on the bay Of Hellefpont all

na - ked ftood, Im - patient of de - lay, He

leapt in - to the fa - - tal flood: The raging

feas, Whom none can pleafe, 'Gainft him their

malice fhow; The heavens lowr'd, The rain

down pour'd, And loud the winds did blow.

Then casting round his eyes,
　Thus of his fate he did complain:
Ye cruel rocks and skies!
　Ye stormy winds, and angry main!
　　What 'tis to miss
　　The lover's bliss,
　Alas! ye do not know;
　　Make me your wreck
　　As I come back,
　But spare me as I go.

Lo! yonder stands the tower
　Where my beloved Hero lies,
And this th' appointed hour
　Which sets to watch her longing eyes.
　　To his fond suit
　　The gods were mute;
　The billows answer, No;
　　Up to the skies
　　The surges rise,
　But sunk the youth as low.

Meanwhile the wishing maid,
　Divided 'twixt her care and love,
Now does his stay upbraid,
　Now dreads he shou'd the passage prove;
　　O fate! said she,
　　Nor heaven nor thee
　Our vows shall e'er divide;
　　I'd leap this wall,
　　Could I but fall
　By my Leander's side.

At length the rifing fun
  Did to her fight reveal, too late,
That Hero was undone;
  Not by Leander's fault, but fate.
        Said fhe, I'll fhew,
        Tho' we are two,
    Our loves were ever one;
        This proof I'll give,
        I will not live,
    Nor fhall he die alone.

Down from the wall fhe leapt
  Into the raging feas to him,
Courting each wave fhe met
  To teach her weary'd arms to fwim:
        The fea gods wept,
        Nor longer kept
    Her from her lover's fide;
        When join'd at laft,
        She grafp'd him faft,
    Then figh'd, embrac'd, and died.

K 2

SONG XXVII.

GRAMACHREE MOLLY.

As down on Banna's banks I ſtray'd, One

even-ing in May, 'The little birds, in blytheſt

notes, Made vo-cal ev'ry ſpray: They ſung their

little tales of love, They ſung them o'er and

o'er; Ah Gramachree, ma Colleenouge, Ma

Mol-ly Aſhtore!

The daify pied, and all the fweets
   The dawn of nature yields;
The primrofe pale, the vi'let blue,
   Lay fcatter'd o'er the fields:
Such fragrance in the bofom lies
   Of her whom I adore.
           Ah Gramachree, &c.

I laid me down upon a bank,
   Bewailing my fad fate,
That doom'd me thus the flave of love,
   And cruel Molly's hate:
How can fhe break the honeft heart
   That wears her in its core?
           Ah Gramachree, &c.

You faid you lov'd me, Molly dear!
   Ah! why did I believe?
Yet, who could think fuch tender words
   Were meant but to deceive?
That love was all I afk'd on earth,
   Nay, heaven could give no more.
           Ah Gramachree, &c.

Oh had I all the flocks that graze
   On yonder yellow hill,
Or low'd for me the num'rous herds
   That yon green pafture fill;
With her I love I'd gladly fhare
   My kine and fleecy ftore.
           Ah Gramachree, &c.

Two turtle doves above my head
   Sat courting on a bough;

I envied not their happinefs,
    To fee them bill and coo:
Such fondnefs once for me fhe fhew'd;
    But now, alas! 'tis o'er.
                    Ah Gramachree, &c.

Then fare thee well, my Molly dear,
    Thy lofs I e'er fhall mourn;
Whilft life remains in Strephon's heart,
    'Twill beat for thee alone:
Tho' thou art falfe, may heav'n on thee
    Its choiceft bleffings pour.
                    Ah Gramachree, &c.

SONG XXVIII.

THE MAID IN BEDLAM.

To the foregoing Tune.

ONE morning very early, one morning in the fpring,
I heard a maid in Bedlam, who mournfully did fing;
Her chains fhe rattled on her hands, while fweetly thus fung
            fhe:
I love my love, becaufe I know my love loves me.

Oh cruel were his parents, who fent my love to fea;
And cruel, cruel was the fhip that bore my love from me:
Yet I love his parents, fince they're his, altho' they've ruin'd
            me;
And I love my love, becaufe I know my love loves me.

Oh fhould it pleafe the pitying pow'rs to call me to the fky,
I'd claim a guardian angel's charge, around my love to fly;
To guard him from all dangers, how happy fhould I be!
For I love my love, becaufe I know my love loves me.

I'll make a ftrawy garland, I'll make it wond'rous fine;
With rofes, lillies, daifies, I'll mix the eglantine;
And I'll prefent it to my love when he returns from fea;
For I love my love, becaufe I know my love loves me.

Oh if I were a little bird, to build upon his breaft!
Or if I were a nightingale, to fing my love to reft!
To gaze upon his lovely eyes, all my reward fhou'd be;
For I love my love, becaufe I know my love loves me.

Oh if I were an eagle, to foar into the fky!
I'd gaze around with piercing eyes, where I my love might
          fpy:
But ah! unhappy maiden! that love you ne'er fhall fee;
Yet I love my love, becaufe I know my love loves me.

SONG XXIX.

THEN SAY, MY SWEET GIRL, CAN YOU LOVE ME?

Andantino.

Dear Nan-cy I've fail'd the world

all a--round, and fe--ven long years

been a ro---ver, To make for my

charmer each fhil--ling a pound, But

now my hard pe--rils are o----ver. I've

fav'd from my toils ma-ny hundreds in gold,

The comforts of life for to get, Have

borne in each climate the heat and the cold, Have

borne in each climate the heat and the cold, And

all for my pret-ty Bru-nette: Then fay, my

fweet girl, can you love me? Then fay, my

fweet girl, can you love me? Then fay, my

fweet girl, can you love me?

L

Tho' others may boaft of more riches than mine,
    And rate my attractions e'en fewer;
At their jeers and ill-nature I'll fcorn to repine,
    Can they boaft of a heart that is truer?
Or, will they for thee plough the hazardous main,
    Brave the feafons both ftormy and wet?
If not, why I'll do it again and again,
    And all for my pretty Brunette.
        Then fay, my fweet girl, &c.

When order'd afar in purfuit of the foe,
    I figh'd at the bodings of fancy,
Which fain wou'd perfuade me I might be laid low,
    And ah! never more fee my Nancy:
But hope, like an angel, foon banifh'd the thought,
    And bade me fuch nonfenfe forget;
I took the advice, and undauntedly fought,
    And all for my pretty Brunette.
        Then fay, my fweet girl, &c.

SONG XXX.

BLACK EYED SUSAN.

All in the Downs the   fleet   was   moor'd,

The ftreamers wa - - ving in the wind,

When black-ey'd Su - - fan came on board;

" Oh! where fhall I my true love find? Tell

me, ye jo - - vial fai - - lors, tell me true,

If my fweet Wil - - liam, if my fweet Wil - liam

fails among your crew.

William, who high upon the yard,
　　Rock'd with the billows to and fro,
Soon as her well-known voice he heard,
　　He figh'd, and caft his eyes below;
The cord flides fwiftly thro' his glowing hands,
And, quick as lightning, on the deck he ftands.

So the fweet lark, high pois'd in air,
　　Shuts clofe his pinions to his breaft,
If chance his mate's fhrill cry he hear,
　　And drops into her welcome neft.
The nobleft captain in the Britifh fleet,
Might envy William's lips thofe kiffes fweet.

O Sufan, Sufan, lovely dear,
　　My vows fhall ever true remain;
Let me kifs off that falling tear,
　　We only part to meet again;
Change as ye lift, ye winds, my heart fhall be
The faithful compafs that ftill points to thee.

Believe not what the landmen fay,
　　Who tempt with doubts thy conftant mind;
They'll tell thee failors, when away,
　　In every port a miftrefs find:
Yes, yes, believe them when they tell thee fo,
For thou art prefent wherefoe'er I go.

If to fair India's coaft we fail,
　　Thy eyes are feen in diamonds bright,
Thy breath's in Afric's fpicy gale,
　　Thy fkin is ivory fo white:
Thus every beauteous object that I view,
Wakes in my foul fome charms of lovely Sue.

Though battle calls me from thy arms,
    Let not my pretty Sufan mourn ;
'Tho' cannons roar, yet fafe from harms,
    William fhall to his dear return.
Love turns afide the balls that round me fly,
Left precious tears fhould drop from Sufan's eye.

The boatfwain gave the dreadful word,
    The fails their fwelling bofom fpread,
No longer muft fhe ftay aboard ;
    They kifs'd, fhe figh'd, he hung his head.
Her lefs'ning boat unwilling rows to land :
Adieu, fhe cries, and wav'd her lily hand.

SONG XXXI.

TAMMY'S COURTSHIP.

Oh where ha'e ye been a' day, my

boy Tammy? Where ha'e ye been a' day,

my boy Tam-my? I've been by burn and

flow'ry brae, Meadow green, and mountain grey,

Courting o' this young thing, juft come frae

her Mammy

And where gat ye that young thing? my boy Tammy.
And where gat ye that young thing? my boy Tammy.
I gat her down in yonder how,
Smiling on a broomy know,
Herding a wee lamb and ewe for her poor Mammy.

What faid ye to that young thing? my boy Tammy.
What faid ye to that young thing? my boy Tammy.
I prais'd her een fae bonny blue,
Her dimpled cheek and cherry mou';
I pree'd it aft, as ye may trow, fhe faid fhe'd tell her Mammy.

I held her to my beating breaft; "My young, fmiling Lammy,
I held her to my beating breaft; "My young, fmiling Lammy,
" I hae a houfe, it coft me dear,
" I've walth o' plenifhin' and gear,
" Ye'fe get it a', war't ten times mair, gin ye will leave your
  " Mammy."

The fmile gade aff her bonny face; " I manna leave my
  " Mammy;
The fmile gade aff her bonny face; " I manna leave my
  " Mammy;
" She's gi'en me meat, fhe's gi'en me claife,
" She's been my comfort a' my days,
" My father's death brought mony waes; I canna leave my
  " Mammy."

" We'll tak' her hame, and mak' her fain, my ain kind-
  " hearted Lammy;
" We'll tak' her hame, and mak' her fain, my ain kind-
  " hearted Lammy;
" We'll gi'e her meat; we'll gi'e her claife;
" We'll be her comfort a' her days;"
The wee thing gi'es her hand, and fays, " There! gang and
  " afk my Mammy.

SONG XXXII.

ALLOA HOUSE.

The ſpring time re-turns, and clothes

the green plains, And Al-lo-a ſhines more

chear--ful and gay; The lark tunes his

throat, and the neighbour-ing ſwains Sing

merrily round me where-e--ver I ſtray;

But San--dy no more re---turns to

my view! No spring time me cheers, no

mu-fic can charm, He's gone; and I

fear me for e--ver a-dieu! A-dieu, ev'ry

pleafure this bo-fom can warm.

O Alloa houfe! how much art thou chang'd!
How filent, how dull to me is each grove!
Alone I here wander where once we both rang'd,
Alas! where to pleafe me my Sandy once ftrove!

M

Here Sandy I heard the tales that you told;
Here liftened, too fond, whenever you fung;
Am I grown lefs fair then, that you are turn'd cold?
Or foolifh, believ'd a falfe, flattering tongue?

So fpoke the fair maid; when forrow's keen pain,
And fhame, her laft fault'ring accents fuppreft:
For fate at that moment brought back her dear fwain,
Who heard, and, with rapture, his Nelly addreft:
My Nelly! my fair, I come; O my Love,
No power fhall thee tear again from my arms,
And, Nelly! no more thy fond fhepherd reprove,
Who knows thy fair worth, and adores all thy charms.

She heard; and new joy fhot thro' her foft frame,
And will you, my love! be true? fhe reply'd;
And live I to meet my fond fhepherd the fame?
Or dream I that Sandy will make me his bride?
O Nelly! I live to find thee ftill kind;
Still true to thy fwain, and lovely as true;
Then adieu to all forrow! what foul is fo blind
As not to live happy for ever with you?

SONG XXXIII.

TAK' YOUR AULD CLOAK ABOUT YE.

In   winter when the rain rain'd cauld,   And

frost and snaw on il - - - - ka hill, And Boreas

wi' his blasts sae bauld, Was threat'ning a' our

ky to kill; Then Bell my wife, who

lo'es nae strife, She said to me right haf-ti-

ly, Get up gudeman, save Crummy's life, And

tak' your auld cloak a-bout ye.

M 2

My Crummy is an useful cow,
    And she is come of a guid kine;
Aft has she wet the bairns mou',
    And I am laith that she should tyne:
Get up, gudeman, it is fu' time,
    The sun shines in the lift sae hie;
Sloth never made a gracious end,
    Gae tak' your auld cloak about ye.

My cloak was anes a guid grey cloak,
    When it was fitting for my wear;
But now its scantly worth a groat,
    For I have worn't this thirty year.
Let's spend the gear that we have won,
    We little ken the day we'll die;
Then I'll be proud, since I have sworn
    To have a new cloak about me.

In days when our king Robert rang,
    His trews they cost but half-a-crown;
He said they were a groat o'er dear,
    And ca'd the taylor thief and lown.
He was the king that wore the crown,
    And thou'rt a man of laigh degree,
'Tis pride puts a' the country down,
    Sae tak' thy auld cloak about ye.

Every land has its ain laugh,
    Ilk kind of corn it has its hool;
I think the warld is a' run wrang,
    When ilka wife her man wad rule.
Do ye not see Rob, Jock, and Hab,
    As they are girded gallantly?

While I fit hurklen in the aic—
  I'll have a new cloak about me.

Gudeman, I wat 'tis thirty years
  Since we did ane anither ken;
And we have had between us twa
  Of lads and bonny laffes ten:
Now they are women grown and men,
  I wifh and pray well may they be;
And if you prove a good hufband,
  E'en tak' your auld cloak about ye.

Bell my wife fhe lo'es nae ftrife,
  But fhe wad guide me if fhe can;
And, to maintain an eafy life,
  I aft maun yield, though I'm gudeman.
Nought's to be won at woman's hand,
  Unlefs ye gi'e her a' the plea:
Then I'll leave aff where I began,
  And tak' my auld cloak about me.

SONG XXXIV.

FAREWELL, DEAR GLENOWEN.

Tune—*Tho' Leixlip is proud, &c.*

Farewell, dear Glen-ow-en! a-dieu to thy

mountains, Where oft I have wander'd to

welcome the day; Farewell to thy · forefts,

thy cry-ftal-line fountains, Which ftray thro'

the val--ley, and moan as they ftray. O'er

wide foamy waters I'm deftin'd to travel, A

poor fimple ex-ile, for-lorn and unknown; Yet

while the dark fates fhall my for---tune un-

ra--vel, My thoughts, my affec-tions fhall

ftill be thy own.

Thy cities, proud Gallia, thy wide-fpreading treafures,
    Thy vallies, where Nature luxuriantly roves,
May bid the heart, dancing to Fancy's wild meafures,
    Forget, for a moment, its own native groves:

But where is the bofom that fighs not in forrow,
    Eftrang'd from dear objects, to wander alone,
Still counting the moments, from morrow to morrow,
    A poor weary traveller, loft and unknown?

Sweet viftas of myrtle, and paths of gay rofes,
    And hills deck'd with vineyards, and woodlands with fhades,
Frefh banks of young vi'lets where fancy repofes,
    And courts gentle flumbers her vifions to aid;
The dark filent grotto, the foft-flowing fountains,
    Where Nature's own mufic flow murmurs along;
The fun-beams that dance on the pine-cover'd mountains
    May waken to rapture their own native throng.

But thou, dear Glenowen! canft bring fweeter pleafure,
    All barren and bleak as thy fummits appear;
And tho' thou canft boaft of no rich gaudy treafure,
    Still memory traces thy charms with a tear!
The keen blafts may howl o'er thy vallies and mountains,
    And ftrip the rich verdure that mantles each tree;
And Winter may bind, in cold fetters, thy fountains,
    And ftill thou art dear, O Glenowen! to me.

SONG XXXV.

MARY'S DREAM.

The moon had climb'd the high--eft

hill, Which ri--fes o'er the fource of Dee,

And from the eaft-ern fam--mit fhed Her

fil--ver light on tow'r and tree;   When

Ma-ry laid her down to fleep, Her

thonghts on San--dy far   at   fea, When

N

soft and low   a   voice   was   heard   say,

Ma - - - ry   weep   no   more   for   me.

She from her pillow gently rais'd
   Her head, to afk who there might be,
She faw young Sandy fhiv'ring ftand,
   With vifage pale and hollow eye:
" O Mary dear, cold is my clay,
   " It lies beneath a ftormy fea,
" Far, far from thee, I fleep in death,
   " So Mary, weep no more for me.

" Three ftormy nights and ftormy days
   " We tofs'd upon the raging main;
" And long we ftrove our bark to fave,
   " But all our ftriving was in vain:
" Ev'n then, when horror chill'd my blood,
   " My heart was fill'd with love for thee:
" The ftorm is paft, and I at reft,
   " So Mary, weep no more for me.

" O maiden dear, thyfelf prepare,
   " We foon fhall meet upon that fhore,
" Where love is free from doubt and care,
   " And thou and I fhall part no more."

Loud crow'd the cock, the fhadow fled,
  No more of Sandy could fhe fee:
But foft the paffing fpirit faid,
  " Sweet Mary, weep no more for me."

SONG XXXVI.

THE SAILOR.

To the foregoing Tune.

OH, ye who fleep on beds of down,
  Who never feel the fting of woe,
Whom Fortune greets with happieft fmiles,
  Whofe hours of varied pleafures flow;
Abfent yourfelves from joy a while,
  And vifit yonder troubled wave;
There view with pain that fatal place;
  It is the common failor's grave!

Surely to him a figh, a tear,
  And fome few tender thoughts are due;
Think that he left the fweets of life,
  To fight—to bleed—to die for you;
His wife, perhaps, (ah! wife no more!)
  Is lift'ning to the hollow blaft,
While hope is whifpering his return,
  Nor knows the hour of death is paft!

Perhaps his little orphans too,
  While playing round their mother's knee,
Have cried, " To-morrow he will come;"
  Oh ne'er will fun THAT morrow fee!

N 2

When they fhall hear—" He comes no more !"
   What bitter moments will they fpend?
'Tis yours to foothe the widow's grief,
   To be the helplefs orphan's friend.

Heedlefs of danger, to the fcene
   Of war the lowly hero came;
There fell unnotic'd, and unknown—
   The world's a ftranger to his name!
Scorn not to think on one fo poor;
   Worth oft adorns the humble mind;
Oft' in a COMMON failor's heart
   Dwell virtues of NO COMMON kind.

SONG XXXVII.

THE TANKARD OF ALE.

Not drunk, nor yet fober, but brother to

both, I met a young man up-on Aylefbery

vale, I faw by his face that he was in

good cafe To come and take fhare of a

tank - ard of ale, la ral la la la ra

la la la ra la la ra la la ra la la

I faw by his face that he was in good

cafe To come and take fhare of a

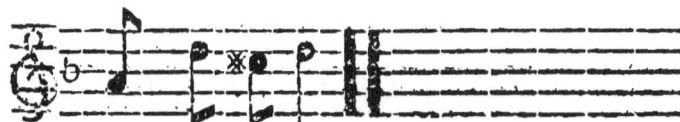

tank - ard of ale.

The hedger who works in the ditches all day,
And labours fo very hard at the plough tail,
He'll talk of great things, about princes and kings,
When once he fhakes hands with a tankard of ale.

The beggar that begs without any legs,
She's fcarce got a rag to cover her tail,
Yet's as merry with rags as a mifer with bags,
When once fhe fhakes hands with a tankard of ale.

The widow that buried her hufband of late,
She's fcarcely forgotten to weep or to wail,
But thinks every day ten till fhe's married again,
When once fhe fhakes hands with a tankard of ale.

The old parifh vicar, when he's in his liquor,
Will merrily at his parifhioners rail,
Come pay all your tithes, or I'll kifs all your wives,
When once he fhakes hands with a tankard of ale.

The old parifh clerk, with his eyes in the dark,
And letter fo fmall that he fcarcely can tell,
He'll read every letter, and fing the pfalms better,
When once he fhakes hands with a tankard of ale.

If wrangling and jangling, or any fuch ftrife,
Or any things elfe may happen to fall,
From words turn to blows and a fharp bloody nofe,
We're friends again over a tankard of ale.

SONG XXXVIII.

THE LASS OF PEATIE'S MILL.

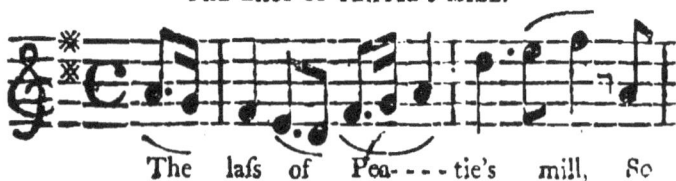

The lafs of Pea- - - - tie's mill, So

bonny blyth and gay, In spite of

all my skill, hath stole my

heart a-way. When tedding of the

hay, Bare--head--ed on the green, Love

midst her locks did play, and wanton'd

in her een.

Her arms, white, round, and smooth;
　　Breasts rising in their dawn;
To age it would give youth,
　　To press them with his hand.
Through all my spirits ran
　　An extacy of bliss,
When I such sweetness fand,
　　Wrapt in a balmy kiss.

Without the help of art,
　　Like flow'rs which grace the wild.
Her sweets she did impart,
　　Whene'er she spoke or smil'd;
Her looks they were so mild,
　　Free from affected pride,
She me to love beguil'd;
　　I wish'd her for my bride.

Oh! had I all that wealth
　　Hopetoun's high mountains fill.
Insur'd long life and health,
　　And pleasure at my will;
I'd promise, and fulfil,
　　That none but bonny she,
The lass of Peatie's mill,
　　Should share the fame with me.

SONG XXXIX.

THE SEA-STORM.

Ceafe, rude Bo - reas, bluft'ring railer, Lift, ye

landf - men, all to me, Mefsmates, hear a

bro - ther failor Sing the dan - - gers of the

fea; From bounding billows firft in motion, When the

diftant whirlwinds rife, To the tempeft troubled

ocean, Where the feas contend with fkies.

O

LIVELY.

Hark! the boatfwain hoarfely bawling,—
  By topfail fheets and haulyards ftand!
Down top-gallants quick be hauling!
  Down your ftay-fails, hand, boys, hand!
Now it frefhens, fet the braces;
  Quick the topfail fheets let go;
Luff, boys, luff, don't make wry faces!
  Up your topfails nimbly clew!

SLOW.

Now all you on down-beds fporting,
  Fondly lock'd in beauty's arms,
Frefh enjoyments wanton courting,
  Free from all but love's alarms,—
Round us roar the tempeft louder;
  Think what fear our mind enthrals:
Harder yet, it yet blows harder;
  Now again the boatfwain calls:

QUICK.

The topfail-yards point to the wind, boys!
  See all clear to reef each courfe!
Let the fore-fheets go; don't mind, boys,
  Though the weather fhould be worfe.
Fore and aft the fpritfail-yard get;
  Reef the mizen; fee all clear:
Hand up! each preventer-brace fet;
  Man the fore-yard, cheer, lads, cheer!

SLOW.

Now the dreadful thunder's roaring!
  Peals on peals contending clafh!
On our heads fierce rain falls pouring!
  In our eyes blue lightnings flafh!

One wide water all around us,
  All above us one black fky!
Diff'rent deaths at once furround us—
  Hark! what means that dreadful cry?

QUICK.

The foremaft's gone, cries every tongue out,
  O'er the lee, twelve feet 'bove deck:
A leak beneath the cheft-tree's fprung out;
  Call all hands to clear the wreck.
Quick the lanyards cut to pieces!
  Come, my hearts, be ftout and bold!
Plumb the well, the leak increafes;
  Four feet water's in the hold!

SLOW.

While o'er the fhip wild waves are beating,
  We for wives or children mourn;
Alas! from hence there's no retreating;
  Alas! from hence there's no return.
Still the leak is gaining on us;
  Both chain-pumps are choak'd below,
Heav'n have mercy here upon us!
  For only that can fave us now!

QUICK.

O'er the lee-beam is the land, boys;
  Let the guns o'er-board be thrown!
To the pump come every hand, boys;
  See our mizen-maft is gone.
The leak we've found; it cannot pour faft:
  We've lighten'd her a foot or more;
Up, and rig a jury fore-maft:
  She rights, fhe rights, boys! wear off fhore.

Now once more on joys we're thinking,
   Since kind Fortune ſpar'd our lives;
Come, the can, boys, let's be drinking
   To our ſweethearts and our wives.
Fill it up, about ſhip wheel it;
   Cloſe to the lips a brimmer join,
Where's the tempeſt now? who feels it?
   None! our danger's drown'd in wine!

SONG XL.

RULE, BRITANNIA.

When Britain firſt, at Heav'n's com-

mand, A-roſe - - - - - - - - - - from out the a-

zure main, Aroſe from out the azure

main, This was the charter, the charter

of the land, And guardian an - - - - - - gels

fung this ftrain : Rule, Bri - tan - nia, Bri-

tannia, rule the waves, Britons ne - - - - - - ver

fhall be flaves.

The nations not fo bleft as thee,
    Muft, in their turns, to tyrants fall ;
    Muft, in their turns, to tyrants fall ;
Whilft thou fhalt flourifh—fhalt flourifh great and free,
    The dread and envy of them all,
        Rule, Britannia, &c.

Still more majeftic fhalt thou rife,
  More dreadful, from each foreign ftroke;
  More dreadful, from each foreign ftroke:
As the loud blaft that—loud blaft that tears the fkies,
  Serves but to root the native oak.
            Rule, Britannia, &c.

Thee haughty tyrants ne'er fhall tame;
  All their attempts to bend thee down,
  All their attempts to bend thee down,
Will but aroufe thy—aroufe thy gen'rous flame,
  But work their woe and thy renown.
            Rule, Britannia, &c.

To thee belongs the rural reign;
  Thy cities fhall with commerce fhine;
  Thy cities fhall with commerce fhine;
And thine fhall be the—fhall be the fubject main;
  And ev'ry fhore it circles, thine.
            Rule, Britannia, &c.

SONG XLI.

ROY'S WIFE OF ALDIVALLOCH.

Roy's wife of Al - di - valloch,   Roy's wife of

Al--di-valloch, Wat ye how she cheated me, As

I came o'er the braes of Bal--loch?

She vow'd she swore she would be mine; She

said she loe'd me best of o--ny; But

ah! the faufe the fic--kle quean, She's ta'en the

carle, and left her Johnnie.

Her hair's fae fair, her een's fae clear,
Her wee bit mou's fae fweet and bonny,
To me fhe ever will be dear,
Tho' fhe's for ever left her Johnnie.
      Roy's wife, &c.

But O, fhe was the canty quean,
And weel could dance the Highland walloch;
How happy I, had fhe been mine,
Or I'd been Roy of Aldivalloch!
      Roy's wife, &c.

SONG XLII.

COME UNDER MY PLAIDY.

Come un - der my plaidy, the night's gaun

to fa', Come in frae the cauld blaft, the

drift and the fnaw; Come under my plaidy, and

lie down beside me, There's room in't, dear

laffie! be---lieve me, for twa,   Come

under my plaidy, and lie down beside me, I'll

hap ye frae ev'ry cauld blaft that will blaw; O come

under my plaidy, and lie down beside me, There's

room in't, dear laffie! be-lieve me, for twa,

" Gae 'wa wi' your plaidy! auld Donald, gae 'wa!
" I fear na' the cauld blaſt, the drift, nor the ſnaw :
" Gae 'wa wi' your plaïdy! I'll no lie beſide ye ;
" Ye might be my gutchard; auld Donald gae 'wa!
" I'm gaun to meet Johnny, he's young and he's bonny ;
" He's been at Meg's bridal, fou trig and fou braw !
" O there's nane dance ſae lightly, ſae gracefu', ſae tightly,
" His cheeks are like roſes, his brow's like the ſnaw."

" Dear Marion, let that ſlee ſtick faſt to the wa',
" Your Jock's but a gowk, and has naething ava' ;
" The hale o' his pack he has now on his back ;
" He's thretty, and I'm but threeſcore and twa.
" Be frank now and kindly : I'll buſk you ay finely ;
" At kirk or at market they'll nane gang ſae braw ;
" A bein houſe to bide in, a chaiſe for to ride in,
" And ſlunkies to 'tend ye as faſt as ye ca'."

" My father ay tell'd me, my mither and a',
" Ye'd mak' a gude huſband, and keep me ay braw ;
" It's true I lo'e Johnny, he's gude and he's bonny,
" But, wae's me ! I ken he has naething ava !
" I ha'e little tocher ; you've made a gude offer ;
" I'm now mair than twenty ; my time is but ſma'!
" Sae gi'e me your plaidy, I'll creep in befide ye,
" I thought ye'd been aulder than threeſcore and twa !"

She crap in ayont him, beſide the ſtane wa',
Whar Johnny was liſt'ning, and heard her tell a'!
The day was appointed, his proud heart it dunted,
And ſtrack 'gainſt his ſide, as if burſting in twa.

He wander'd hame weary, the night it was dreary,
And thowlefs, he tint his gate deep 'mang the fnaw;
The howlet was fcreaming, while Johnny cried, " Women
" Wad marry Auld Nick, if he'd keep them ay braw."

O the deil's in the laffes! they gang now fae braw,
They'll lie down wi' auld men o' four-fcore and twa;
The hale o' their marriage is gowd and a carriage;
Plain luve is the cauldeft blaft now that can blaw!
But lo'e them 1 canna, nor marry I winna,
Wi' ony daft laffie! tho' fair as a queen;
Till love ha'e a fhare o't, the never a hair o't
Shall gang in my wallet at morning or e'en.

SONG XLIII.

THE RAILERS.

Behold on the brow the leaves play in the

breeze, While cattle calm feed in the vale;

The church spire ta‑pering points thro' the

trees, As lord of the hill and the

dale. The playful colts skip af‑ter dams to the

brook, The brook flow and fi-lently glides; The

fur-face fo fmooth and fo clear, If you

look it reflects the gay green on its

fide -

It reflects the gay green on its fide.

In farm-yard, by his feather'd feraglio carefs'd,
   The king of the walk dares to crow;
No nabob, nor Nimrod, enflaving the eaft,
   Such prowefs with beauty can fhew.

Beneath the ſtill cow, Nancy preſſes the teat,
  Her face like the ruddy-fac'd morn;
Loud ſtrokes in the barn the ſtrong threſhers repeat,
  Or winnow for market the corn.

Induſtrious, their wives, at the doors of their cots,
  Sit ſpinning, dreſs'd cleanly, tho' coarſe;
To their babes, while unheeding the traveller trots,
  They ſhew the fine man and his horſe.
At the heels of the ſteed bark the baſe village whelps,
  Each puppy rude echo beſtirs,
But the horſe, too high bred, bounds away from their yelps,
  Diſregarding the clamour of curs.

Illiberal RAILERS thus envy betray,
  When merit above them they view;
But Genius diſdains to turn out of his way,
  Or afford a reply to the crew.
To contempt and deſpair, ſuch inſanes we commit;
  But to generous rivals a toaſt,—
May rich men reward honeſt fellows of wit,—
  Here's a health to thoſe dunces hate moſt.

SONG XLIV.

THE AUCTION MORALIZED.

That fleeting are our deareſt joys, phi-

lo-ſophers have taught, But who would think that

Auction-Halls were with ſuch wiſdom fraught?

At-tend a lit-tle to my ſong, and I'll

re-veal to thee, How ſages all and

hamm'ring call ſo, wond'rouſly a---gree.

Harmoniouſly mingling here, the works of ages lie;
Here, Wit and Fancy's faireſt flow'rs, and truths that never die:
Repoſing in their letter'd tombs, the wits of Greece and Rome
    Mementos give, that ſome may laugh, and others mourn their
    doom.
Here's Sophiſtry wire-woven, bound, and Piety in ſheets,
Hypocriſy, whoſe gilded caſe, the gazer's eye ſoon meets:
Here ſtands the judge, with lifted arm, his juſtice to diſpenſe;
But ne'er decides without a bribe—ſtill tries their weight in
    pence.
Now throng the hall both great and ſmall, of high and low
    degree,
And ſage and ſavage cluſter'd cloſe, as buds are on a tree:
Some come their empty heads to fill, ſome in the way of trade;
Others their libraries to ſtore, their fortunes being made:
Some, from the plenteous ſhow of weeds, a few ſweet flow'rs
    to cull;
And ſome for learning, to reduce, the thickneſs of their ſkull.
The "Book of Sports," with ſmiling face, the judge diſplays
    to view;
Now bid! he cries, how ſweet in youth, when ev'ry thing
    is new!
The younkers bid, and faſter bid, till once! twice!!
    thrice!!! 'tis gone,
As quickly as the morning ray, which on us lately ſhone.
"Imagination's Pleaſures" now, are open'd to their eyes,
And many bid, but going! gone!! they ſink, no more to riſe.
Though Virgil and though Homer bring their heroes to their
    aid,
Yet, going! going! gone! at laſt they vaniſh in the ſhade.
Demoſthenes and Cicero are next expos'd to ſale,
And, who would not be eloquent? to bid you cannot fail!

But orators and statesmen too can't stand the hammer's stroke,
For presto! gone! they fleet away, as does the passing joke.
To " Histories" of Nations all, both savage and refin'd,
" The Ruins of Empires" soon succeed, and blot them from
   the mind.
" The World," at length, embellished with heads, and pressed
   hot,
Is pompously exhibited, and styl'd a precious lot.
Now bid at once a hundred tongues, each other to outstrip;
A few draw back and meditate, left they should make a slip.
Lo! tumult's all throughout the hall, till gone! at last they
   hear;
The sound is like the cannon's roar, that thunders on the ear.

☞ The above song may likewise be sung to the Tune of—
  " There was a jolly miller once," &c.

Q

SONG XLV.

THE LAST TIME I CAME O'ER THE MUIR.

The laſt time I came o'er the muir, I

left my love be--hind me: Ye pow'rs

what pain do I endure, When ſoft

i--de---as mind me. Soon as the

ruddy morn diſplay'd, the beaming day en-

fuing, I met betimes my love---ly maid

In fit re---treats for woo-ing.

Beneath the cooling shade we lay,
    Gazing and chastely sporting;
We kiss'd and promis'd time away,
    'Till night spread her black curtain.
I pitied all beneath the skies,
    Ev'n kings, when she was nigh me;
In raptures I beheld her eyes,
    Which could but ill deny me.

Should I be call'd where cannons roar,
    Where mortal steel may wound me;
Or cast upon some foreign shore,
    Where dangers may surround me;
Yet hopes again to see my love,
    To feast on glowing kisses,
Shall make my care at distance move,
    In prospect of such blisses.

In all my soul there's not one place
    To let a rival enter;
Since she excels in every grace,
    In her my love shall centre.

Sooner the feas fhall ceafe to flow,
 Their waves the Alps fhall cover;
On Greenland's ice fhall rofes grow,
 Before I ceafe to love her.

The next time I gang o'er the muir,
 She fhall a lover find me;
And that my faith is firm and pure,
 Though I left her behind me.
Then Hymen's facred bands fhall chain
 My heart to her fair bofom;
There, while my being does remain,
 My love more frefh fhall bloffom.

SONG XLVI.

O SAY, BONNY LASS

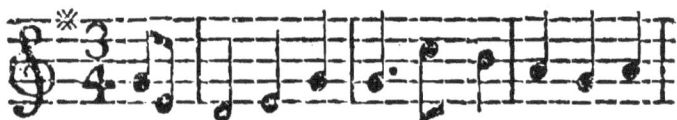

O fay, bonny lafs, will you ly in a

barrack? And marry a fodger, and car-ry his

wallet? O fay, will you leave baith your

mammy and daddy, And go to the wars

with your fodg---er lad--die? O

fay, will you leave baith your mammy and

daddy, And go to the wars with your

fodg---er laddie?

O yes, bonny lad, I will ly in a barrack,
And marry a fodger, and carry his wallet;
I'll neither afk leave of my mammy nor daddy,
But aff and away with my dear fodger laddie.

O fay, bonny lafs, will you go a campaigning?
And bear all the hardfhips of battle and famine?
When wounded and bleeding, then wilt thou draw near me?
And kindly fupport me, and tenderly cheer me?

O yes, I will brave all thefe perils you mention,
And twenty times more, if you had the invention;
Neither hunger, nor cold, nor dangers alarm me,
While I have my Harry, my deareft to charm me.

SONG XLVII.

INKLE AND YARICO.

To the foregoing Tune.

INKLE.

O SAY, fimple maid, have you form'd any notion
Of all the rude dangers in croffing the ocean?
When winds whiftle fhrilly, ah! won't they remind you
To figh with regret for the grot left behind you?

YARICO.

Ah! no, I could follow, and fail the world over,
Nor think of my grot, when I look at my lover!
The winds which blow round us, your arms for my pillow,
Will lull us to fleep, whilft we're rock'd by each billow.

INKLE.

Then fay, lovely lafs, what if haply efpying
A rich gallant veffel with gay colours flying?

YARICO.

I'll journey with thee, love, to where the land narrows,
And fling all my cares at my back with my arrows."

BOTH.

O fay then, my true love, we never will funder,
Nor fhrink from the tempeft, nor dread the loud thunder;
Whilft conftant, we'll laugh at all changes of weather,
And journey all over the world both together.

SONG XLVIII.

I'LL NEVER LEAVE THEE.

One day I heard Mary fay, How fhall I

leave thee? Stay, deareft A ---- donis, ftay,

Why wilt thou grieve me? A-

las, my fond heart will break, If thou

fhould leave me! I'll live and die

for thy fake, Yet ne--ver leave thee.

Say, lovely Adonis, fay,
    Has Mary deceiv'd thee?
Did e'er her young heart betray,
    New love to grieve thee?
My conftant mind ne'er fhall ftray,
    Thou mayft believe me;
I'll love thee, lad, night and day,
    And never leave thee.

Adonis, my charming youth,
    What can relieve thee?
Can Mary thy anguifh foothe,
    This breaft fhall receive thee.
My paffion can ne'er decay,
    Never deceive thee:
Delight fhall drive pain away,
    Pleafure revive thee.

But leave thee, lad, leave thee, lad,
    How fhall I leave thee?
O! that thought makes me fad;
    I'll never leave thee.
Where would my Adonis fly?
    Why does he grieve me?
Alas! my poor heart will die,
    If I fhould leave thee.

SONG XLIX.

TWEED-SIDE.

What beauties does Flora dif - - clofe! How

fweet are her fmiles up - - on Tweed! Yet

Mary's ftill fweet - er than thofe, Both

Nature and Fancy ex - - - ceed. No

dai - fy, nor fweet blufh - ing rofe, Nor

R

all the gay flow'rs of the field, Nor

Tweed glid -- ing gent - ly 'thro' thofe, Such

beau - ty and plea - fure does yield.

The warblers are heard in the grove,
   The linnet, the lark, and the thrufh,
The blackbird and fweet cooing dove,
   With mufic enchant every bufh.
Come, let us go forth to the mead,
   Let us fee how the primrofes fpring;
We'll lodge in fome village on Tweed,
   And love while the feather'd folks fing.

How does my love pafs the lang day ?
   Does Mary not tend a few fheep?
Do they never carelefsly ftray,
   While, happily, fhe lies afleep?

Tweed's murmurs fhould lull her to reft;
  Kind nature indulging my blifs,
To relieve the faft pains of my breaft,
  I'd fteal an ambrofial kifs.

'Tis fhe does the virgins excel,
  No beauty with her may compare;
Love's graces around her do dwell:
  She's faireft, where thoufands are fair.
Say, charmer, where do thy flocks ftray?
  Oh! tell me at noon where they feed;
Shall I feek them on fweet winding Tay,
  Or pleafanter banks of the Tweed?

SONG L.

JENNY DANG THE WEAVER.

At Wil-ly's wed-ding on the green,

The laf--fes, bonny witches, Were a' dreft out

in aprons clean, And braw white Sunday mutches:

Auld Mag-gy bade the lads tak' tent, But Jock

would not believe her; But foon the fool his

fol - ly kent, For Jen - - ny dang the weaver.

CHORUS.

Jenny dang, dang, dang, Jen - ny dang the

weaver; But foon the fool his fol - ly kent,

For Jenny dang the weaver.

At ilka country dance or reel,
  Wi' her he would be bobbing;
When fhe fat down, he fat down,
  And to her would be gabbing;
Where'er fhe gade, baith but and ben,
  The coof wou'd never leave her,
Ay keckling like a clocking hen,
  But Jenny dang the weaver,
    Jenny dang, &c.

Quo' he, " My lafs, to fpeak my mind,
  " In troth I needna fwither,
" You've bonny een, and if ye're kind,
  " I'll never feek anither?"
He humm'd and haw'd; the lafs cried peugh!
  And bade the coof no deave her;
Syne fnapt her fingers, lap and leugh,
  And dang the filly weaver.
        And Jenny dang, dang, dang,
          Jenny dang the weaver;
        Syne fnapt her fingers, lap and leugh,
          And dang the filly weaver.

SONG LI.

HOW STANDS THE GLASS AROUND?

How ftands the glafs around? For fhame ye

take no care, my boys, How ftands the glafs a-

round? Let mirth and wine a - - bound. The

trum - - pets found, The co - lours they are

flying, boys, To fight, kill, or wound, May

we ftill be found Content with our hard

fate, my boys, On the cold ground.

Why, foldiers, why,
Should we be melancholy, boys?
Why, foldiers, why?
Whofe bufinefs 'tis to die!

What, fighing? fie!
Don't fear, drink on, be jolly, boys!
'Tis he, you, or I!
Cold, hot, wet, or dry,
We're always bound to follow, boys,
And fcorn to fly!

'Tis but in vain,—
I mean not to upbraid you, boys,—
'Tis but in vain,
For foldiers to complain:
Should next campaign
Send us to him who made us, boys,
We're free from pain!
But if we remain,
A bottle and kind landlady
Cure all again.

SONG LII.

PINKIE HOUSE.

By Pin--kie Houfe oft let me walk,

While cir--cled in my arms, I hear

my Nel-ly sweet--ly talk, And gaze o'er

all her charms. O let me e-ver

fond behold Those gra--ces void of

art! Those cheer-ful smiles that sweet--ly

hold In will---ing chains my heart.

S

O come, my love, and bring anew
    That gentle turn of mind;
That gracefulneſs of air, in you,
    By nature's hand deſign'd:
That beauty, like the bluſhing roſe,
    Firſt lighted up this flame!
Which, like the ſun, for ever glows
    Within my breaſt the ſame.

Ye light coquets! ye airy things!
    How vain is all your art!
How ſeldom it a lover brings!
    How rarely keeps a heart!
O gather from my Nelly's charms,
    That ſweet, that graceful eaſe;
That bluſhing modeſty that warms;
    That native art to pleaſe!

Come then, my love, O! come along,
    And feed me with thy charms;
Come, fair inſpirer of my ſong,
    O fill my longing arms!
A flame like mine can never die,
    While charms, ſo bright as thine,
So heav'nly fair, both pleaſe the eye,
    And fill the ſoul divine.

SONG LIII.

ANNA'S URN.

Encompafs'd in an angel's frame, An

an-gel's vir-tues lay:. Too foon did heav'n

af-fert its claim, And call'd its own a-

way, and call'd its own a-way.

My An-na's worth, my An-na's charms Can

never more return, Can never more re-

turn! What then shall fill these widow'd arms?

Ah --------- me! Ah me! Ah me!

my An-na's Urn!

Can I forget that bliss refin'd,
    Which, blest with her, I knew?
Our hearts, in sacred bonds entwin'd,
    Were bound by love too true.
That rural train, which once were us'd
    In festive dance to turn,
So pleas'd, when Anna they amus'd,
    Now weeping deck her Urn.

The soul escaping from its chain,
    She clasp'd me to her breast,
  " To part with thee is all my pain!"
    She cried, then sunk to rest!

While mem'ry ſhall her ſeat retain,
   From beauteous Anna torn,
My heart ſhall breathe its ceaſeleſs ſtrain.
   Of ſorrow o'er her Urn.

There, with the earlieſt dawn, a dove
   Laments her murder'd mate :
There Philomela, loſt to love,
   Tells the pale moon her fate.
With yew and ivy round me ſpread,
   My Anna there I'll mourn;
For all my ſoul, now ſhe is dead,
   Concentres in her Urn.

SONG LIV.

THE BROOM OF THE COWDENKNOWS.

How blyth was I each morn to fee, My

fwain come o'er the hill! He leap'd the

brook, and flew to me; I met him with

good will. O, the broom, the bonny bonny

broom, The broom of the Cow-denknows; I

wish I were with my dear swain, With

his pipe and my ewes.

I neither wanted ewe nor lamb,
    When his flocks round me lay;
He gather'd in the sheep at night,
    And cheer'd me all the day.
        O, the broom, &c.

He tun'd his pipe and reed so sweet,
    The birds sat list'ning by;
The fleecy sheep stood still and gaz'd,
    Charm'd with his melody.
        O, the broom, &c.

While thus we spent our time by turns,
    Betwixt our flocks and play;
I envy'd not the fairest dame,
    Though e'er so rich and gay.
        O, the broom, &c.

He did oblige me ev'ry hour,
 Cou'd I but faithful be?
He ftole my heart, cou'd I refufe
 Whate'er he afk'd of me?
   O, the broom, &c.

Hard fate that I muft banifh'd be,
 Gang heavily and mourn,
Becaufe I lov'd the kindeft fwain
 That ever yet was born.
   O, the broom, the bonny bonny broom,
   Where laft was my repofe:
   I wifh I were with my dear fwain,
   With his pipe and my ewes,

SONG LV.

GUARDIAN ANGELS.

Andante.

Guardian an-gels, now pro-tect me,

Send, ah! fend, the youth I love:

Deign, O Cu--pid, to di---rect me,

Lead me thro' the myr-----tle grove.

Bear my fighs, foft float---ing air,

Say I love him to--------defpair;

Tell him 'tis for him I grieve, For

him a--lone I wifh to live.

T

'Mid fecluded dales I'll wander,
 Silent as the fhades of night,
Near fome bubbling rill's meander,
 Where he erft has bleft my fight:
There to weep the night away,
There to wafte in fighs the day,
Think, fond youth, what vows you fwore,
And muft I never fee thee more?

Then reclufe fhall be my dwelling,
 Deep in fome fequefter'd vale;
There, with mournful cadence fwelling,
 Oft repeat my love-fick tale.
And the Lark and Philomel
Oft fhall hear a virgin tell,
What the pain to bid adieu
To joy, to happinefs, and you.

SONG LVI.

JOCKEY'S RETURN.

The ither morn, when I forlorn, Aneath an

aik fat moaning, I didna trow I'd fee my jo Be-

fide me gin the glowming; But he fu' trig,

lap o'er the rig, And dawtingly did cheer me, When

I, whatreck! did leaft expect To fee my lad-

die near me.

His bonnet he, a thought a-jee,
   Cock'd fpruce, when firft he clafp'd me;
And I, I wat, wi' fainnefs grat,
   While in his grips he prefs'd me.
Deil tak' the war! I late and air
   Have wifh'd, fince Jock departed,
But now as glad I'm wi' my lad,
   As fhortfyne broken-hearted.

Fu' aft at e'en, wi' dancing keen,
   When a' were blyth and merry,
I car'd na by, fae fad was I,
   In abfence of my deary.
But praife be blefs'd! my mind's at reft,
   I'm happy wi' my Johnny;
At kirk and fair I'fe ay be there,
   And be as canty's ony.

SONG LVII.

COOLUN.

O the hours I have pafs'd in the

arms of my dear, Can ne--ver

he thought of but with a sad tear!

Oh! for---bear, Oh! for------bear then

to men---tion her name, It re-

calls to my mem'-ry the caufe

of my pain.

How often to love me fhe fondly has fworn,
And when parted from me would ne'er ceafe to mourn;
All hardfhips for me fhe would cheerfully bear,
And at night on my bofom forget all her care.

To fome diftant climate together we'll roam,
And forget all the hardfhips we meet with at home;
Fate, now be propitious, and grant me thine aid,
Give me my Paftora, and I'm more than repaid.

SONG LVIII.

FAIR SALLY.

Hearty.

Fair Sal-ly lov'd a bonny feaman, With

tears fhe fent him out to roam, Young Thomas

lov'd no other woman, But left his heart with

her at home. She view'd the sea from off the

hill, And while she turn'd the spinning

wheel, Sung of her bonny seaman.

The winds blew loud, and she grew paler,
  To see the weather-cock turn round,
When lo! she spied her bonny sailor
  Come singing o'er the fallow ground:
With nimble haste he leap'd the style,
And Sally met him with a smile,
      And hugg'd her bonny sailor.

Fast round the waste he took his Sally,
  But first around his mouth wip'd he,
Like home-bred spark he could not dally,
  But kiss'd and press'd her with a glee:
Thro' winds and waves and dashing rain,
Cry'd he, thy Tom's return'd again,
      And brings a heart for Sally.

Welcome! fhe cried, my conftant Thomas,
    Tho' out of fight, ne'er out of mind;
Our hearts tho' feas have parted from us,
    Yet they my thoughts did leave behind:
So much my thoughts took Tommy's part,
That time nor abfence from my heart
            Could drive my conftant Thomas.

This knife, the gift of lovely Sally,
    I ftill have kept for her dear fake;
A thoufand times, in am'rous folly,
    Thy name I've carv'd upon the deck.
Again this happy pledge returns,
To tell how truly Thomas burns,
            How truly burns for Sally.

This thimble didft thou give to Sally,
    Whilft this I fee I think of you;
Then why does Tom ftand fhilly fhally,
    While yonder fteeple's in our view?
Tom, never to occafion blind,
Now took her in the coming mind,
            And went to church with Sally.

SONG LIX.

SWEET ANNIE.

Sweet Annie frae the fea-beach came,

Where Jock-ey fpeel'd the vef--fel's fide, Ah!

wha can keep their heart at hame, When

Jockey's toft a---boon the tide. Far

aff to dif---tant realms he gangs,

U

Yet I'll prove true as he has

been; And when ilk lafs a - - - - bout him

thrangs, He'll think on An - - - nie, his

faith - - - ful ane.

I met our wealthy laird yeftreen,
   Wi' goud in hand he tempted me,
He prais'd my brow, my rolling een,
   And made a brag of what he'd gi'e.
What though my Jockey's far away,
   Toft up and down the awfome main,
I'll keep my heart anither day,
   Since Jockey may return again.

Nae mair, falfe Jamie, fing nae mair,
    And fairly caft your pipe away;
My Jockey wad be troubled fair,
    To fee his friend his love betray:
For a' your fongs and verfe are vain,
    While Jockey's notes do faithful flow:
My heart to him fhall true remain,
    I'll keep it for my conftant jo.

Blaw faft, ye gales, round Jockey's head,
    And gar your waves be calm and ftill;
His hameward fail with breezes fpeed,
    And dinna a' my pleafure fpill.
What tho' my Jockey's far away,
    Yet he will braw in filler fhine;
I'll keep my heart anither day,
    Since Jockey may again be mine.

U 2

SONG LX.

KATE OF DOVER.

Pompofo.

Ned Flint was lov'd by all the fhip, Was

ten---der hearted, bold and true, He'd

work his way, or drink his flip, With e'er a

fea--man in the crew; Tho' Ned had

fac'd his country's foe, And twice had fail'd the

world all o-ver, Had seen his messmates

oft laid low, Yet would he sigh, yet would he

sigh for Kate of Dover.

Fair was the morn', when on the shore,
Ned flew to take of Kate his leave,
Says he, My love your grief give o'er,
For Ned can ne'er his Kate deceive.
Let Fortune smile, or let her frown,
To you I ne'er will prove a rover,
All cares in generous flip I'll drown,
And still be true to Kate of Dover.

The tow'ring cliffs they bade adieu,
To brave all dangers on the main,
When lo! a sail appear'd in view,
And Ned with many a tar was slain.

Thus death, who lays each forrow low,
Robb'd Kitty of her faithful lover,
The tars oft tell the tale of woe,
And heave a figh for Kate of Dover.

SONG LXI.

SHE 'ROSE AND LET ME IN.

The night her filent fa---ble wore, And

gloo-my were the fkies; Of glitt'ring ftars

appear'd ro more than thofe in Nel--ly's

eyes.   When   to   her fa - ther's   door

I came, Where I had of --- ten been,   I

begg'd my fair, my love ---- ly dame, To

rife and let   me in.

But fhe, with accents all divine,
    Did my fond fuit reprove;
And while fhe chid my rafh defign,
    She but inflam'd my love.
Her beauty oft had pleas'd before,
    While her bright eyes did roll:
But virtue only had the pow'r
    To charm my very foul.

Then who would cruelly deceive,
　Or from such beauty part?
I lov'd her so, I could not leave
　The charmer of my heart.
My eager fondness I obey'd,
　Resolv'd she should be mine,
'Till Hymen to my arms convey'd
　My treasure so divine.

Now happy in my Nelly's love,
　Tranfporting is my joy:
No greater bleffing can I prove,
　So blefs'd a man am I:
For beauty may a while retain
　The conquer'd flutt'ring heart;
But virtue only is the chain
　Holds, never to depart.

MARY OF CASTLE-CARY.

Plaintive.

Saw ye my wee thing? faw ye mine

ain thing? Saw ye my true love down

by yon lee? Crofs'd fhe the meadow, yef-

treen at the gloaming? Sought fhe the

burnie, whar flow'rs the haw-tree?

X

" Her hair it is lint-white! her skin it is milk-white!
    " Dark is the blue of her saft rolling e'e!
" Red, red her ripe lip is, and sweeter than roses!
    " Whar could my wee thing wander frae me?"

' I saw na your wee thing, I saw na your ain thing,
    ' Nor saw I your true love down by yon lee;
' But I met my bonny thing late in the gloaming,
    ' Down by the burnie, whar flow'rs the haw-tree.

' Her hair it was lint-white, her skin it was milk-white,
    ' Dark was the blue o' her saft rolling e'e!
' Red war her ripe lips, and sweeter than roses;
    ' Sweet war the kisses that she gae to me!'

" It was na my wee thing! it was na mine ain thing!
    " It was na my true love ye met by the tree!
" Proud is her liel heart, and modest her nature,
    " She never loo'd Le-man till ance she loo'd me.

" Her name it is Mary, she's frae Castle-Cary,
    " Aft has she sat, when a bairn, on my knee!
" Fair as your face is, war't fifty times fairer,
    " Young braggart, she ne'er wad gi'e kisses to thee!"

' It was then your Mary, she's frae Castle-Cary,
    ' It was then your true love I met by the tree!
' Proud as her heart is, and modest her nature,
    ' Sweet war the kisses that she gae to me!'

Sair gloom'd his dark brow, blood-red his cheek grew,
    Wild flash'd the fire frae his red rolling e'e;

" Ye's rue fair this morning, your boasting and scorning;
  " Defend, ye faufe traitor, for loudly ye lie!"

' Awa wi' beguiling,' then cried the youth smiling;
  Aff gaed the bonnet; the lint-white locks flee;
The belted plaid fa'ing, her white bofom shawing,
  Fair stood the lov'd maid wi' the dark rolling e'e!

" Is it my wee thing? is it mine ain thing?
" Is it my true love here that I fee?"
    ' O Jamie! forgi'e me, your heart's conftant to me;
    ' I'll never mair wander, my true love, frae thee.'

X 2

SONG LXIII.

DAINTIE DAVIE.

Lively.

The lasses fain wad ha'e frae me, A

fang to keep them a' in glee, While ne'er a

ane I ha'e to gi'e, But on-ly Dain-tie

Da - - vie. I learn'd it ear - - ly in my

youth, When barley bannocks caus'd a drouth, Wha

cronics met to weet their mouth, Our

fang was Dain---tie Da---vie.

CHORUS.

O, Dain-tie Da--vie is the thing, I

ne--ver kent a can--ty fpring, That

e'er de-ferv'd the high---lan' fling, Sae

weel as Dain--tie Da--vie.

When fiiends an' fouk at bridals meet,
Their drouthy mou's and craigs to weet,
The ſtory canna be complete
   Without they've Dainty Davie.
Sae ladies tune your ſpinnets weel,
An' lilt it up wi' a' your ſkill,
There's nae ſtrathſpey nor highlan' reel,
   Comes up to Daintie Davie.
      O, Daintie Davie, &c.

Tho' bardies a', in former times,
Ha'e ſtain'd my ſang, wae-worth their rhymes!
They had but little menſe wi' crimes,
   To blaſt my Daintie Davie.
The rankeſt weeds the garden ſpoil,
When labour tak's the play a while,
The lamp gaes out for want o' oil,
   And ſae it far'd wi' Davie.
      O, Daintie Davie, &c.

There's ne'er a bar but what's complete,
While ilka note is ay ſae ſweet,
That auld an' young get to their feet,
   When they hear Daintie Davie.
Until the lateſt hour of time,
When muſic a' her pow'r ſhall tine,
Each hill, an' dale, an' grove ſhall ring,
   Wi' bonny Dainty Davie.
      O, Daintie Davie, &c.

SONG LXIV.

THE YELLOW HAIR'D LADDIE.

Slow.

In April, when Primroſ-es paint the

ſweet plain, And ſummer ap--proach-ing re-

joic--eth the ſwain, joic-eth the ſwain,

The yel---low-hair'd lad-die would

of--ten-times go, To wilds and deep

glens, where the haw - thorn trees grow,

hawthorn trees grow.

There, under the fhade of an old facred thorn,
With freedom he fung his loves evening and morn,
He fung with fo foft and enchanting a found,
That Sylvans and Fairies unfeen danc'd around.

The fhepherd thus fung: Tho' young Maddie be fair,
Her beauty is dafh'd with a fcornful proud air:
But Sufie was handfome, and fweetly could fing;
Her breath, like the breezes, perfum'd in the fpring.

That Maddie, in all the gay bloom of her youth,
Like the moon, was inconftant, and never fpoke truth:
But Sufie was faithful, good-humour'd, and free,
And fair as the goddefs that fprung from the fea.

That mamma's fine daughter, with all her great dow'r,
Was awkwardly airy, and frequently four:
Then, fighing, he wifh'd, would parents agree,
The witty, fweet Sufan, his miftrefs might be.

' SONG LXV.

EWE-BUGHTS, MARION.

Will ye go to the ewe-bughts, Marion, And

wear in the sheep wi' me? The sun shines

sweet, my Marion, But nae half sae sweet as

thee. The sun shines sweet, my Marion, But

nae half sae sweet as thee,

O Marion's a bonny lafs,
  And the blyth blink's in her e'e;
And fain wad I marry Marion,
  Gin Marion wad marry me.

There's goud in your garters, Marion,
  And filk on your white haufe-bane:
Fu' fain wad I kifs my Marion,
  At e'en when I come hame.

I've nine milk ewes, my Marion,
  A cow and a brawny quey,
I'll gi'e them a' to my Marion,
  Juft on her bridal day.

And ye's get a green fey apron,
  And waiftcoat of the London brown,
And vow but ye will be vap'ring,
  Whene'er ye gang to the town.

I'm young and ftout, my Marion;
  Nane dances like me on the green;
And gin ye forfake me, Marion,
  I'll e'en draw up wi' Jean.

Sae put on your pearlins, Marion,
  And kyrtle of the cramafie!
And foon as my chin has nae hair on,
  I fhall come weft, and fee thee.

SONG LXVI.

To the foregoing Tune.

HOW blyth' have I been with my Sandy,
  As we fat in the how o' the glen!
But nae mair can I meet wi' my Sandy,
  To the banks o' the Rhine he has gane.

Alas! that the trumpet's loud clarion,
  Thus draws a' our fhepherds afar,
O could not the ewe-bughts and Marion,
  Pleafe mair than the horrors of war?

Not a plough in our land has been ganging,
  The oufen ha'e ftood in their fta':
Nae flails in our barns ha'e been banging,
  For mair than this towmond or twa.

Wae's me, that the trumpet's fhrill clarion,
  Thus draws a' our fhepherds afar!
O I wifh that the ewe-bughts and Marion
  Could charm from the horrors of war.

SONG LXVII.

SWEET ELLEN.

Andante.

Cold blew the wind, no gleam of light, When

El - - - len left her home, And

brav'd the horrors of the night, o'er dreary

wilds to roam, O'er drea - - ry wilds to

roam. The love - ly maid had late been

gay, When hope and plea - - fure fmil'd,

But now ,a - - las! to grief a prey, Was

El - - len, for - - row's child, Was El - len,

for - - row's child.

She long was William's promis'd bride,
  But ah! how fad her doom!
The gentle youth, in beauty's pride,
  Was fummon'd to the tomb.
No more thofe joys fhall Ellen prove,
  Which many an hour beguil'd;
From morn to eve fhe mourns her love,
  Sweet Ellen, forrow's child.

With falt'ring ftep away fhe flies,
  O'er William's grave to weep;

For Ellen there, with tears and fighs,
    Her watch would often keep.
The pitying angel faw her woe,
    And came with afpect mild;
Thy tears fhall now no longer flow,
    Sweet Ellen, forrow's child.

Thy plaintive notes were heard above,
    Where thou fhalt foon find reft;
Again thou fhalt behold thy love,
    And be for ever bleft.
Ah! can fuch blifs be mine! fhe cried,
    With voice and looks fo wild;
Then funk upon the earth and died,
    Sweet Ellen, forrow's child.

SONG LXVIII.

MARIA.

'Twas near a thicket's calm re - - treat,

Under a pop - - lar tree, Ma - ri - - a

chofe her lone--ly feat, To mourn her

forrows free. Her love--ly form was

fweet to view, As dawn at op'ning day;

But ah! fhe mourn'd her love not true, And

wept her cares a--way.

The brook flow'd gently at her feet,
 In murmurs fmooth along;
Her pipe, which once fhe tun'd fo fweet,
 Had now forgot its fong.

No more to charm the vale fhe tries,
　　For grief has fill'd her breaft;
Fled are the joys fhe us'd to prize,
　　And fled with them her reft.

Poor haplefs maid! who can behold
　　Thy anguifh fo fevere,
Or hear thy love-lorn ftory told,
　　Without a pitying tear!
Maria, haplefs maid, adieu!
　　Thy forrows foon muft ceafe;
Soon heaven will take a maid fo true
　　To everlafting peace.

SONG LXIX.

BRAES OF BALLENDINE.

Be - - - neath a green fhade a

lovely young fwain, One ev'ning re-

clin'd to dif - - - - - co - - - - - ver his

pain: So   fad, yet   fo   fweetly,   he

warbled   his   woe,   The   wind ceas'd   to

breathe,   And   the   foun - - tains   to

flow;   Rude   winds with   com - - paffion   could

hear   him   com - plain,   Yet   Chloe   lefs

gentle,   was   deaf   to   his   ftrain.

Z,

How happy, he cry'd, my moments once flew,
E'er Chloe's bright charms firſt flaſh'd on my view!
Thoſe eyes, then, with pleaſure, the dawn could ſurvey,
Nor ſmil'd the fair morning more cheerful than they;
Now ſcenes of diſtreſs pleaſe only my ſight,
I ſicken in pleaſure, and languiſh in light.

Thro' changes, in vain, relief I purſue:
All, all but conſpire my griefs to renew:
From ſunſhine, to zephyrs and ſhades we repair;
To ſunſhine we fly from too piercing an air:
But love's ardent fever burns always the ſame!
No winter can cool it, no ſummer inflame.

But, ſee! the pale moon, all clouded, retires!
The breezes grow cool, not Strephon's deſires!
I fly from the dangers of tempeſt and wind,
Yet nouriſh the madneſs that preys on my mind.
Ah, wretch! how can life be worthy thy care,
Since length'ning its moments but lengthens deſpair

SONG LXX.

THE GRACEFUL MOVE.

Moderato.

When firſt I ſaw thee graceful move,

Ah! me, what meant my throb‑bing

breaſt; Say; ſoft con‑‑‑‑fu‑‑‑ſion,

art thou love? If love thou

art, then fare‑‑‑well reſt.

Z 2

With gentle fmiles affuage the pain,
Thofe gentle fmiles did firft create,
And though you cannot love again,
In pity, ah! forbear to hate.

SONG LXXI.

'TWAS WHEN THE SEAS WERE ROARING.

'Twas when the feas were roar-ing With

hollow blafts of wind, A damfel lay de-

plor-ing, All on a rock reclin'd.   Wide

o'er the rolling billows, She caft a wifhful

look; Her head was crown'd with wil-

lows, That trembled o'er the brook.

Twelve months were gone and over,
    And nine long tedious days;
Why didst thou, vent'rous lover,
    Why didst thou trust the seas?
Ceafe, ceafe, thou troubled ocean,
    And let my lover reft;
Ah! what's thy troubled motion
    To that within my breaft?

The merchant, robb'd of treafure,
    Views tempefts with defpair;
But what's the lofs of treafure,
    To lofing of my dear?
Should you fome coaft be laid on,
    Where gold and diamonds grow,
You'd find a richer maiden,
    But none that loves you fo.

How can they fay that nature
    Has nothing made in vain?
Why then, beneath the water
    Do hideous rocks remain?

No eyes the rocks difcover
　　That lurk beneath the deep,
To wreck the wand'ring lover,
　　And leave the maid to weep.

Thus melancholy lying,
　　Thus wail'd fhe for her dear;
Repaid each blaft with fighing,
　　Each billow with a tear:
When o'er the white waves ftooping,
　　His floating corpfe fhe fpied;
Then, like a lily drooping,
　　She bow'd her head,—and died.

SONG LXXII.

BUSH ABOON TRAQUAIR.

Hear me, ye nymphs, and ev'----ry

fwain, I'll tell how Peg--gy grieves me; Tho'

thus I languish and com-plain, A--las she

ne'er be-lieves me: My vows and

sighs, like si--lent air, Un--heed--ed

ne---ver move her, The bon--ny

bush a----boon Tra-quair, Was where I

first did love her.

That day fhe fmil'd and made me glad;
　　No maid feem'd ever kinder;
I thought myfelf the luckieft lad,
　　So fweetly there to find her.
I try'd to foothe my am'rous flame,
　　In words that I thought tender;
If more there pafs'd I'm not to blame;
　　I meant not to offend her.

Yet now fhe fcornful flees the plain,
　　The fields we then frequented;
If e'er we meet fhe fhows difdain,
　　She looks as ne'er acquainted.
The bonny bufh bloom'd fair in May,
　　Its fweets I'll ay remember;
But now her frowns make it decay;
　　It fades as in December.

Ye rural pow'rs, who hear my ftrains,
　　Why thus fhould Peggy grieve me?
Oh, make her partner in my pains!
　　And let her fmiles relieve me!
If not, my love will turn defpair;
　　My paffion no more tender;
I'll leave the bufh aboon Traquair;
　　To lonely wilds I'll wander.

SONG LXXIII.

THE HIGHLAND LADDIE.

The lawland lads think they are fine, But

oh they're vain and id --- ly gawdy; How

much un - - like the grace - fu' mein, And

man - ly looks of my Highland lad - die.

O my bonny Highland laddie, my handsome

smiling Highland laddie, May heav'n still guard,

and love reward, The lawland lass and her

Highland laddie.

If I were free at will to chufe,
   To be the wealthieft lawland lady,
I'd take young Donald without trews,
   With bonnet blue, and belted plaidy.
            O my bonny, &c.

The brawest beau in burrow's town,
   In a' his airs, with art made ready,
Compar'd to him he's but a clown;
   He's finer far in's tartan plaidie.
            O my bonny, &c.

O'er benty hill with him I'll run,
   And leave my lawland kin and daddy,
Frae winter's cauld, and fummer's fun,
   He'll screen me with his Highland plaidy.
            O my bonny, &c.

A painted room and filken bed,
   May pleafe a lawland laird and lady;
But I can kifs and be as glad,
   Behind a bufh in's Highland plaidy,
              O my bonny, &c.

Few compliments between us pafs,
   I ca' him my dear Highland laddie,
And he ca's me his lawland lafs,
   Syne rows me in beneath his plaidy.
              O my bonny, &c.

Nae greater joy I'll e'er pretend,
   Than that his love prove true and fteady,
Like mine to him, which ne'er fhall end,
   While heav'n preferves my Highland laddie.
              O my bonny, &c.

SONG LXXIV.

THE HIGHLAND LASSIE.

To the foregoing Tune.

THE lawland maids gang trig and fine,
   But aft they're four and unco faucy;
Sae proud, they never can be kind,
  . Like my good-humour'd Highland laffie.
      O my bonny Highland laffie,
      My hearty, fmiling Highland laffie,
      May never care make thee lefs fair,
      But bloom of youth ftill blefs my laffie.

Than ony lafs in burrow's-town,
   Wha mak' their cheeks with patches mottie,
I'd tak' my Katty butt a gown,
   Bare-footed in her little coatie
            O my bonny, &c.

Beneath the brier or brecken bufh,
   Whene'er I kifs and court my dawtie,
Happy and blyth as ane wad wifh,
   My flighterin' heart gangs pittie pattie.
            O my bonny, &c.

O'er higheft heathery hills I'll ften,
   With cockit gun and ratches tenty,
To drive the deer out of their den,
   To feaft my lafs on difhes dainty.
            O my bonny, &c.

There's nane shall dare, by deed or word,
  'Gainst her to wag a tongue or finger,
While I can weild my trusty sword,
  Or frae my side whisk out a whinger.
           O my bonny, &c.

The mountains clad with purple bloom,
  And berries ripe, invite my treasure .
To range with me; let great fowk gloom,
  While wealth and pride confound their pleasure.
           O my bonny, &c.

SONG LXXV.

OLD TOWLER.

Bright chanticleer proclaims the dawn, And

spangles deck the thorn; The lowing herd now

quits the lawn, The lark springs from the

corn: Dogs, huntſmen, round the window

throng, Fleet Towler leads the   cry;   A-

riſe   the   bur - den   of   their   ſong,   This

day a ſtag   muſt   die: With   a   hey   ho

chi - - vy, Hark forward, hark   forward tan-

ti - vy, With a   hey ho   chi - vy, Hark forward,

hark forward tanti-vy, Hark forward, hark

forward, hark forward, hark forward tan-

tivy, tantivy, Hark, hark, hark forward, hark

forward tantivy. A----rife the burden

of their fong, This day a ftag muft die; This

day a ftag muft die, This day a ftag muft

die.

The cordial takes its merry round,
    The laugh and joke prevail,
The huntfman blows a jovial found,
    The dogs fnuff up the gale:
The upland winds they fweep along,
    O'er fields through brakes they fly;
The game is rous'd, too true the fong,
    This day a ftag muft die,
                    With a hey ho chiry, &c.

Poor ftag, the dogs thy haunches gore,
    The tears run down thy face;
The huntfman's pleafure is no more,
    His joys were in the chace:
Alike the fportfmen of the town,
    The virgin game in view,
Are full content to run them down,
    Then they in turn purfue.
                    With a hey ho chiry, &c.

SONG LXXVI.

GIN A BODY MEET A BODY.

Gin a bo - dy meet 'a bo - dy Comin

thro' the rye, Gin a bo - dy kiſs a bo - dy,

Need a bo - - dy cry? Il - ka bo - dy has

a bo - dy, Ne'er a ane ha'e I; But

a' the lads they lo'e me weel, And what the

war am I?

B b

Gin a body meet a body
  Comin frae the well,
Gin a body kifs a body,
  Need a body tell?
Ilka body has a body,
  Ne'er a ane hae I;
But a' the lads they lo'e me weel,
  And what the war am I?

Gin a body meet a body
  Comin frae the town,
Gin a body kifs a body,
  Need a body gloom?
Ilka Jenny has her Jockey,
  Ne'er a ane hae I;
But a the lads they lo'e me weel,
  And what the war am I?

SONG LXXVII.

Original words of the foregoing Tune.

COMIN through the rye, poor body,
  Comin through the rye,
She draigl't a' her petticotie,
  Comin through the rye.
Oh Jenny's a' weet, poor body,
  Jenny's feldom dry,
She draigl't a her petticotie,
  Comin through the rye.

Gin a body meet a body
  Comin through the rye,
Gin a body kiſs a body,
  Need a body cry?
     O Jenny's a' weet, &c.

Gin a body meet a body
, Comin through the glen;
Gin a body kiſs a body,
  Need the warld ken?
     Oh Jenny's a' weet, &c.

Kiſſin is the key of love,
  And clappin is the lock,
And makin o's the beſt thing
  That e'er a young thing got.
     Oh Jenny's a' weet, &c;

SONG LXXVIII.

CAROLINE OF LITCHFIELD.

Affetuofo.

The village hind with toil had done, And

homewards bent his way, While

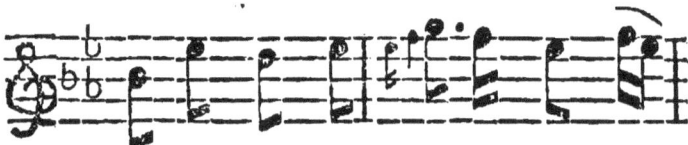

on the wave the fetting fun Clos'd

the de-part-ing day, Clos'd the de-

part--ing day; When Ca-ro-line of

Litchfield ſtrove all ſeem - ing - - ly to

borrow The plaintive wail - ings of the

dove, To aid a while her ſor - row, The

plain - tive wail - ings of the dove, To

aid a while her ſor - - row.

As dews diſtilling on the roſe,
  In brightneſs oft appear;
So Caroline, amid her woes,
  Seem'd lovelier with a tear.

" Ah me !" fhe cried, " life has no charms,
   " For, 'neath the drooping willow,
" My lover fleeps in death's cold arms,
   " Upon a moiften'd pillow.

" For me he brav'd the dang'rous part,
   " And found a watery tomb,
" Can filence reign then in the heart,
   " Or gratitude be dumb ?
" Ah, no! affection's tear fhall flow,
   " Pure as the cryftal fountain,
" Till death fhall end this life of woe,
   " Which now's beyond furmounting."

Then fighing with a wifhful look,
   A loofe to grief fhe gave,
And headlong plung'd into the brook,
   There funk beneath the wave.
The village maids the tale relate,
   At eve aud early morning,
How love was nipt by adverfe fate,
   Ere fcarcely it was dawning.

SONG LXXIX.

BONNY DUNDEE.

O   whar gat ye that bon - - ny blue

bonnet? O fil-ly blind bo-dy, can-na

ye fee? I gat it frae a

bon-ny Scots Callan, Atween St. Johnfton and

bonny Dundee. And O! gin I faw but the

laddie that gae me't, Fu' aft has he doudled me

on o' his knee; But now he's a-wa, and I

dinna ken whar he's; O! gin he war back

to his Minny and me.

My heart has nae room when I think on my dawty,
His dear rofy haffets bring tears in my e'e;
But now he's awa, and I dinna ken whar he's,
Gin we cou'd anfe meet, we's ne'er part till we die.
And O! gin I faw but my bonny Scots Callan,
Fu' aft has he doudled me on his knee;
But now he's away, and I dinna ken whar he's,
O! gin he was back to his Minny and me.

SONG LXXX.

Tune—*Braw lads o' Galla water.*

Ma-ry's charms fub-du'd my breaft, Her

glowing youth, her manner winning, My

faithful vows I fond---ly prefs'd, And mark'd

the fweet re--turn be--ginning.

Fancy kindly on my mind,
  Yet paints that ev'ning's dear declining,
When raptur'd firft I found her kind,
  Her melting foul to love refigning.

C c

Years of nuptial blifs have roll'd,
　　And ftill I've found her more endearing;
Each wayward paffion fhe controul'd,
　　Each anxious care, each forrow cheering.

Children now in ruddy bloom,
　　With artlefs look attention courting,
With infant fmiles difpel each gloom,
　　Around our hut fo gaily fporting.

SONG LXXXI.

BRAW, BRAW LADS ON YARROW BRAES.

To the foregoing Tune.

BRAW, braw lads on Yarrow braes,
　　Ye wander through the blooming heather;
But Yarrow braes, nor Ettrick fhaws,
　　Can match the lads o' Galla water.

But there is ane, a fecret ane,
　　Aboon them a' I lo'e him better,
And I'll be his, and he'll be mine,
　　The bonny lad o' Galla water.

Although his daddie was nae laird,
    And though I ha'e nae meikle tocher,
Yet rich in kindeſt, trueſt love,
    We'll tent our flocks by Galla water.

It ne'er was wealth, it ne'er was wealth,
    That coft contentment, peace, or pleaſure;
The bands and bliſs o' mutual love,
    O that's the chiefeſt warld's treaſure.

Cc 2

SONG LXXXII.

THE SONS OF THE CLYDE.

Tune—*Rural Felicity.*

A - way with proud France and her tyrant

Di - rec - tors, Who make both Re - - ligion and

Vir - tue their sport, Their threats are de - spis'd

by Bri - tannia's protectors, 'Tis Freedom that

calls to her aid and support.   Bri - tannia

demands our hearts and our hands, A - way, let

us conquer or fall. by her fide: Come, fee

Courage and Li - berty no - bly in - fpir - ing the

fons of the Clyde.

'Twas Liberty gave us our commerce and treafure,
　　She taught us to cultivate fcience and mirth,
To patronize learning and focial pleafure,
　　To lighten the heart, and give jollity birth:
Come, come Britons all, it is Liberty's call,
　　Let's hafte to her fhrine, let us garlands provide;
　　　　　Come, fee
　　　　　Courage and Liberty,
Nobly infpiring the fons of the Clyde.

By Freedom we hold all our foes in defiance,
  The banner of Britain o'er earth fhe's unfurl'd,
And fovereigns of nations now court her alliance,
  The terror of ftates, and the pride of the world.
Long, long o'er our ifle may Liberty fmile,
  And blefs her with monarchs us wifely to guide:
        Come, fee
        Courage and Liberty,
  Nobly infpiring the fons of the Clyde.

Make happy, ye fair ones, thofe heroes of fpirit,
  Who've courage and freedom the land to defend;
Be partial to valour, to worth, and to merit,
  For who well deferves you but Liberty's friend?
To guard love and beauty we make it our duty,
  To aid their felicity ftill be our pride:
        Come, fee
        Daughters of Liberty
  Greeting, with rapture, the fons of the Clyde.

SONG LXXXIII.

DOWN THE BURN, DAVIE.

When trees did bud, · and fields

were green, And broom bloom'd fair to

fee, When Ma - - - - ry was com-

plete fifteen, And love laugh'd in her

e'e, Blyth Da - - vie's blinks her heart did

move, To fpeak her mind thus free, Gang

down the burn, Davie, love, down the burn

Davie, love, down the burn, Davie, love, and

I will follow thee, down the burn, Davie, love,

down the burn, Davie, love, down the burn, Davie,

love, Gang down the burn, Davie, love, And

I will follow thee.

Now Davie did each lad furpaſs
  That dwelt on this burn ſide;
And Mary was the bonnieſt laſs,
  Juſt meet to be his bride.
       .Blyth Davie's blinks, &c.

Her cheeks were rofy, red and white,
 Her e'en were bonny blue,
Her looks were like Aurora bright,
 Her lips like dropping dew.
   Blyth Davie's blinks, &c.

What pafs'd, I guefs, was harmlefs play,
 And nothing fure unmeet;
For, ganging hame, I heard them fay,
 They lik'd a walk fo fweet.
   Blyth Davies blinks, &c.

His cheeks to hers he fondly laid;
 She cry'd, " Sweet love, be true;
" And when a wife, as now a maid,
 " To death I'll follow you."
   Blyth Davie's blinks, &c.

As fate had dealt to him a routh,
 Straight to the kirk he led her,
There plighted her his faith and truth,
 And a bonny bride he made her.
No more afham'd to own her love,
 Or fpeak her mind thus free;
" Gang down the burn, Davie, love,
 " And I will follow thee."

SONG LXXXIV.

THE FLOWERS OF THE FOREST.

I've heard of a lilt - - - - ing at

our ewes milk - - - ing, Laſ - - ſes a'

lilt - - ing before the break of day; But

now there's a moan - ing on il - - ka green

loaning, That our braw fo - - reſ - ters are

tr.

a' wede a - way.　　At bughts, in the

morning, nae blyth lads are scorn - ing, The

laf - - - ses are lone - ly, dow - - - ie, and wae;

Nae daf - - - fin, nae gabbin, but sigh - ing and

sab - bing, Ilk ane lifts her leg - - lin, and

tr.

hies her a - way.

At e'en at the gloaming, nae fwankies are roaming
   'Mangft ftacks, with the laffes at bogle to play,
But ilk ane fits dreary, lamenting her deary,
   The flowers of the foreft that are wede away.
At har'ft, at the fheering, nae younkers are jeering,
   The ban'fters are runkled, lyart, and grey;
At a fair or a preaching, nae wooing, nae fleeching,
   Since our braw forefters are a' wede away.

O dool for the order fent our lads to the border!
   The Englifh, for ance, by guile gat the day;
The flowers of the foreft, that ay fhone the foremoft,
   The prime of our land lies cauld in the clay.
We'll hear nae mair lilting at our ewes milking,
   The women and bairns are dowie and wae,
Sighing and moaning on ilka green loaning,
   Since our braw forefters are a' wede away.

SONG LXXXV.

To the foregoing Tune.

I'VE feen the fmiling of fortune beguiling;
   I've felt all its favours, and found its decay;
Sweet was its blefling, kind its careffing,
   But now it is fled—fled far away.

I've feen the foreft adorned the foremoft
 With flowers of the faireft, moft pleafant and gay;
Sae bonny was their blooming, their fcent the air perfuming,
 But now they are withered, and weeded away.

I've feen the morning with gold the hills adorning,
 And loud tempeft ftorming before the mid-day;
I've feen Tweed's filver ftreams fhining in the funny beams,
 Grow drumly and dark as they roll'd on their way.
O fickle fortune! why this cruel fporting?
 O why ftill perplex us, poor fons of a day?
Nae mair your fmiles can cheer me, nae mair your frowns
         can fear me,
 For the flowers of the foreft are withered away.

SONG LXXXVI.

ALONE BY THE LIGHT OF THE MOON.

The day is de-parted, and round from

the cloud The moon in her beau-ty ap-

pears; The voice of the night--ingale

warbles a-loud, The mu--fic of love

in our ears, Ma-ri-a appear! now the

fea - fon fo fweet With the beat of the heart

is in tune; The time is fo ten - der

for lovers to meet A - lone by the light

of the moon, A - lone by the light of

the moon, A - - lone by the light of the

moon, A - lone by the light of the moon,

A - - - - - lone by the light of the

moon.

I cannot, when prefent, unfold what I feel;
  I figh—can a lover do more?
Her name to the fhepherds I never reveal,
  Yet I think of her all the day o'er.
Maria, my love! do you long for the grove,
  Do you figh for an interview foon;
Does e'er a kind thought run on me as you rove,
  Alone by the light of the moon?

Your name from the fhepherds, whenever I hear,
  My bofom is all in a glow;
Your voice, when it vibrates fo fweet thro' mine ear,
  My heart thrills—my eyes overflow.
Ye pow'rs of the fky! will your bounty divine
  Indulge a fond lover his boon;
Shall heart fpring to heart, and Maria be mine,
  Alone by the light of the moon?

SONG LXXXVII.

AMANDA.

Un-lefs with my A--man-da bleft, In

vain I twine the woodbine bow'r; Un-

lefs to deck her fweet-er breaft, In vain

I rear the breath-ing flow'r. A-

waken'd by the genial year, In vain the

E e

birds a-round me fing, In vain the

frefh'ning fields ap-.pear; With---out my

love there is no fpring.

SONG LXXXVIII.

To the foregoing Tune.

YE banks and braes of bonny Doun,
How can ye bloom fo frefh and fair?
How can ye chant, ye little birds,
While I'm fo wae and fu' o' care?
Ye'll break my heart ye little birds,
That wanton through the flowering thorr.;
Ye mind me of departed joys,
Departed, never to return.

Oft have I roam'd by bonny Doun,
To see the rose and woodbine twine,
Where ilka bird sung o'er its note,
And cheerfully I join'd with mine.
Wi' heartsome glee I pull'd a rose,
A rose out of yon thorny tree;
But my false love has stoln the rose,
And left the thorn behind to me.

Ye roses blaw your bonny blooms,
And draw the wild birds by the burn;
For Luman promis'd me a ring,
And ye maun aid me should I mourn:
Ah! na, na, na, ye needna mourn,
My een are dim and drowsy worn;
Ye bonny birds ye needna sing,
For Luman never can return.

My Luman's love, in broken sighs,
At dawn of day by Doun ye'se hear,
And mid-day, by the willow green,
For him I'll shed a silent tear.
Sweet birds, I ken ye'll pity me,
And join me wi' a plaintive sang,
While echo wakes, and joins the mane-
l-mak' for him I loe'd sae lang.

SONG LXXXIX.

LITTLE THINKS THE TOWNSMAN'S WIFE.

Lit-tle thinks the towns-mans wife,

While at home she tar - - - - - - ries,

What must be the laf - - - fie's life, Who a

fol - - - dier mar - - - ries; Now with wea - ry

march - - - - ing spent, Dancing now be-

fore the tent; Li --- ra li -- ra la,

li -- ra li -- ra la, With her jol --- ly

fol --- dier.

In the camp at night fhe lies,
Wind and weather fcorning,
Only griev'd her love muft rife,
And quit her in the morning;
But the doubtful fkirmifh done,
Blyth fhe fings at fet of fun,
Lira lira la, lira lira la,
With her jolly foldier.

Should the captain of her dear
Ufe his vain endeavour,
Whifp'ring nonfenfe in her ear,
Two fond hearts to fever;

At his paſſion ſhe will ſcoff;
Laughing ſhe will put him off,
Lira lira la, lira lira la,
For her jolly ſoldier.

SONG XC.

QUEEN MARY'S LAMENTATION.

I ſigh and lament me in vain, Theſe

walls can but e - - - cho my moan; A-

las, it in - - - creaſes my pain, When I

think of the days that are gone: Thro' the

grate of my pri--fon, I fee The

birds as they wan-ton in air, My

heart how it pants to be free! My

looks they are wild with de-

Above, tho' oppreſt by my fate,
  I burn with contempt for my foes,
'Tho' fortune has alter'd my ſtate,
  She ne'er can ſubdue me to thoſe.
Falſe woman! in ages to come
  Thy malice deteſted ſhall be;
And when we are cold in the tomb,
  Some heart ſtill will ſorrow for me.

Ye roofs where cold damps and diſmay,
  With ſilence and ſolitude dwell,
How comfortleſs paſſes the day,
  How ſad tolls the evening bell;
The owls from the battlements cry,
  Hollow wind ſeems to murmur around,
" O Mary, prepare thee to die,"
  My blood it runs cold at the ſound.

SONG XCI.

TAM GLEN.

My heart is a breaking, dear Tittie, Some

counſel un-to me come len', To an-ger

them a' were a pi-ty, But what will I

do wi' Tam Glen? I'm thinking wi'

ſic a braw fallow, In poortith I might mak'

a fen; What care I in rich - es to

wallow, If I manna mar - ry Tam Glen?

What care I in rich - es to wallow, If

I manna marry Tam Glen.

There's Lowrie the laird o' Dumeller
   ' Gude day to you brute,' he comes ben,
He brags and he blaws o' his filler,
   But when will he dance like Tam Glen?
My Minnie does conftantly deave me,
   And bids me beware o' young men;
They flatter, fhe fays, to deceive me,
   But wha can think fae o' Tam Glen?
       They flatter, &c.

My Daddie fays gin I'll forfake him,
  He'll gi'e me gude hunder marks ten,
But if it's ordain'd I maun tak' him,
  O wha will I get but Tam Glen?
Yeftreen, at the valentines dealing,
  My heart to my mou' gaed a ften,
For thrice I drew ane without failing,
  And thrice it was written, Tam Glen.
        For thrice I drew, &c.

The laft hallowe'en I was wauking
  My drouket fark-fleeve, as ye ken,
His likenefs cam' up the houfe ftauking,
  And the very grey breeks o' Tam Glen.
Come counfel, dear Tittie, don't tarry;
  I'll gi'e you my bonnie black hen,
Gif ye will advife me to marry,
  The lad I lo'e dearly, Tam Glen.
        Gif ye will, &c.

SONG XCII.

TOPSAILS SHIVER IN THE WIND.

The topsails shi - - - ver   in   the   wind, The

ship   she   casts   to   sea;   But   yet   my

soul,   my   heart,   my   mind,   are,   Ma - - - ry,

moor'd   with   thee.   For   tho'   thy   sai-

lor's   bound   a - - far,   Still   love   shall   be   his

lead - ing ftar;   For though   thy   fai - lor's

bound a - - far,   Still   love   fhall   be   his

lead - - - - ing   ftar.

Should landmen flatter when we're fail'd,
 O doubt their artful tales;
No gallant failor ever fail'd,
 If love breath'd conftant gales;
Thou art the compafs of my foul,
Which fteers my heart from pole to pole.

Sirens in every port we meet,
 More fell than rocks or waves;
But fuch as grace the Britifh fleet,
 Are lovers and not flaves:
No foes our courage fhall fubdue,
Altho' we've left our hearts with you.

Thefe are our cares,—but if you're kind,
    We'll fcorn the dafhing main,
The rocks, the billows, and the wind,
    The power of France and Spain :
Now England's glory refts with you,
Our fails are full, fweet girls, Adieu !

SONG XCIII.

THE YOUNG LAIRD AND EDINBURGH KATY.

Now wat ye wha I met yeftreen,

Coming down the ftreet, my joe? My miftrefs

in her tar-tan fcreen, Fu' bonnie, braw and

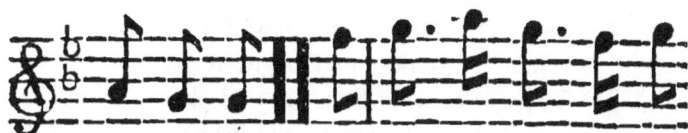

fweet, my joe.   My dear, quoth I, thanks to

the night, That never wifh'd a lover   ill, Since

ye're out of your mither's fight, Let's tak' a wauk

up to   the hill.

O Katy, wiltu' gang wi' me,
　　And leave the dinfome town a while,
The bloffom's fprouting frae the tree,
　　And a' the fimmer's gawn to fmile:
The mavis, nightingale, and lark,
　　The bleating lambs and whiftling hind,
In ilka dale, green fhaw, and park,
　　Will nourifh health, and glad ye'r mind.

Soon as the clear gudeman of day
   Inhales his morning draught of dew,
We'll gae to fome burn-fide and play,
   And gather flow'rs to bufk ye'r brow :
We'll pu' the daifies on the green,
   The lucken gowans frae the bog;
Between hands, now and then we'll lean
   And fport upo' the velvet fog.

There's up into a pleafant glen,
   A wee piece frae my father's tow'r,
A canny, faft, and flow'ry den,
   Where circling birks have form'd a bower :
Whene'er the fun grows high and warm,
   We'll to that cauler fhade remove,
There will I lock thee in my arms,
   And love and kifs, and kifs and love.

SONG XCIV.

KATH'RINE OGIE.

Slow.

As walk-ing forth to view the plain,

Up--on a morn-ing ear---ly, While

May's sweet scent did cheer my brain, From

Flow'rs which grow so rare-ly: I

chanc'd to meet a pret--ty maid, She

G g

shin'd though it was fo - - - - gie, I

afk'd her name: Sweet Sir, fhe faid, My

name is Kath'rine Ogie.

I ftood a while, and did admire,
　To fee a nymph fo ftately;
So brifk an air there did appear
　In this dear maid fo neatly.
Such nat'ral fweetnefs fhe difplay'd,
　Like lillies in a bogie;
Diana's felf was ne'er array'd
　: Like this fame Kath'rine Ogie.

Thou flow'r of females, beauty's queen,
　Who fees thee, fure muft prize thee;
Tho' thou art drefs'd in robes but mean,
　Yet thefe cannot difguife thee:

Thy handfome air and graceful look,
　　Excels a clownifh rogie;
Thou'rt match for laird, or lord, or duke,
　　My charming Kath'rine Ogie.

O were I but fome fhepherd fwain;
　　To feed my flock befide thee,
At bughting-time to leave the plain,
　　In milking to abide thee;
I'd think myfelf a happier man,
　　With Kate, my club, and dogie,
Than he that hugs his thoufands ten,
　　Had I but Kath'rine Ogie.

Then I'd defpife th' imperial throne,
　　And ftatefmen's dang'rous ftations;
I'd be no king, I'd wear no crown,
　　I'd fmile at conqu'ring nations;
Might I carefs and ftill poffefs
　　This lafs of whom I'm vogie;
For thefe are toys, and ftill look lefs,
　　Compar'd with Kath'rine Ogie.

I fear the gods have not decreed
　　For me fo fine a creature,
Whofe beauty rare makes her exceed
　　All other works in nature.
Clouds of defpair furround my love,
　　That are both dark and fogie:
Pity my cafe, ye pow'rs above,
　　I die for Kath'rine Ogie.

SONG XCV.

HENRY'S COTTAGE MAID.

Ah, where can fly my soul's true

love? Sad I wan - - der this

lone grove; Sighs and tears for

him I fhed, Hen - - - - ry is from

Lau - - - - - ra fled. Thy love

to   me   thou didſt im‑‑part, Thy

love   ſoon   won   my   vir‑‑‑‑‑‑gin.

heart: But, dear.‑eſt Henry, thou'ſt be‑

tray'd   Thy ‑‑‑‑ love with thy poor

cot‑tage   maid.

Through the vale my grief appears,
Sighing ſad, with pearly tears:
Oft thy image is my theme,
As I wander on the green:

See, from my cheek the colour flies,
And love's fweet hope within me dies;
For oh! dear Henry, thou'ft betray'd
Thy love, with thy dear village maid.

SONG XCVI.

THE MILLER.

Slowifh.

O mer-ry may the maid be That

marries with the mil-ler, For foul

day and fair day, He's ay bringing

till her. Has ay a pen-ny in his

purfe, For dinner and for fup-per; And,

gin fhe pleafe, a good fat cheefe, And lumps

of yellow butter.

When Jamie firft did woo me,
   I fpeir'd what was his calling;
Fair maid, fays he, O come and fee,
   Ye're welcome to my dwalling:
Though I was fhy, yet I could fpy
   The trnth of what he told me,
And that his houfe was warm and couth,
   And room in it to hold me.

Behind the door a bag of meal,
   And in the kift was plenty
Of good hard cakes his mither bakes,
   And bannocks were na fcanty;
A good fat fow, a fleeky cow
   Was ftanding in the byre;
Whilft lazy pufs with mealy moufe
   Was playing at the fire.

Good figns are thefe, my mither fays,
   And bids me tak' the miller;
For foul day and fair day
   He's ay bringing till her;
For meal and malt fhe does na want,
   Nor ony thing that's dainty;
And now and then a keckling hen,
   To lay her eggs in plenty.

In winter, when the wind and rain
   Blaws o'er the houfe and byre,
He fits befide a clean hearth ftane,
   Before a roufing fire;
With nut-brown ale he tells his tale,
   Which rows him o'er fu' nappy;
Who'd be a king!—a petty thing,
   When a miller lives fo happy.

SONG XCVII.

KIND ROBIN LO'ES ME.

Andantino.

Ro--bin is my on---ly jo, For

Ro--bin has the art to lo'e, So

to his fuit I mean to bow, Be-caufe

I ken he lo'es me. Hap-py, hap-py

was the fhow'r, That led me to his

H h

birk - en bow'r, Where firſt of love I - .

fand the pow'r, And kend that Ro - bin

lo'e'd me.

They ſpeak of napkins, ſpeak of rings,
Speak of gloves and kiſſing-ſtrings,
And name a thouſand bonny things,
  And ca' them ſigns he lo'es me:
But I'd prefer a ſmack of Rob,
Seated on the velvet fog,
To gifts as lang's a plaiden wab,
  Becauſe I ken he lo'es me.

He's tall and ſonſy, frank and free,
Loe'd by a' and dear to me,
Wi' him I'd live, wi' him I'd die,
  Becauſe my Robin lo'es me.

My Titty Mary faid to me,
Our courtfhip but a joke wad be,
And I, ere lang, be made to fee,
   That Robin did nae lo'e me.

But little kens fhe what has been
Me and my honeft Rob between,
And in his wooing, O fae keen
   Kind Robin is that lo'es me.
Then fly ye lazy hours away,
And haften on the happy day,
When ' join your hands,' Mefs John fhall fay,
   And mak' him mine that lo'es me.

Till then, let ev'ry chance unite,
To weigh our love and fix delight,
And I'll look on a' fuch wi' fpite,
   Wha doubt that Robin lo'es me.
O hey, Robin, quo' fhe,
O hey, Robin, quo' fhe,
O hey, Robin, quo' fhe,
   Kind Robin lo'es me.

SONG XCVIII.

THE DISCONSOLATE SAILOR.

When my mo-ney was gone, that I

gain'd in the wars, And the world 'gan to

frown on my fate, What matter'd my zeal,

or my ho - - nour - - ed fcars, When in-

dif - - ference ftood at each gate.

The face that would fmile when my purfe was well lin'd,
  Shew'd a different afpect to me;
And when I could nought but ingratitude find,
  I hied once again to the fea.

I thought it unwife to repine at my lot,
  Or to bear with cold looks on the fhore,
So I pack'd up the trifling remnants I'd got,
  And a trifle, alas! was my ftore.

A handkerchief held all the treafure I had,
  Which over my fhoulder I threw,
Away then I trudg'd, with a heart rather fad,
  To join with fome jolly fhip's crew.

The fea was lefs troubled by far than my mind,
  For when the wide main I furvey'd,
I could not help thinking the world was unkind,
  And Fortune a flippery jade :

And vow'd, if once more I could take her in tow,
  I'd let the ungrateful ones fee,
That the turbulent winds and the billows could fhew
  More kindnefs than they did to me,

SONG XCIX.

UNGRATEFUL NANNY.

Allegretto.

Did e---ver fwain a nymph a-dore, As

I un--grate-ful Nan--ny do? Was

e--ver fhepherd's heart fo fore, Was

e-ver bro-ken heart fo true? My

cheeks are fwell'd with tears, but fhe Has

ne - - ver fhed a tear for me; My

cheeks are fwell'd with tears, but fhe Has

never fhed a tear for me.

If Nanny call'd, did Robin ftay,
    Or linger when fhe bid me run?
She only had the word to fay,
    And all fhe afk'd was quickly done:
I always thought on her, but fhe
Would ne'er beftow a thought on me.
        I always thought, &c.

To let her cows my clover tafte,
    Have I not rofe by break of day?
When did her heifers ever faft,
    If Robin in his yard had hay?
Tho' to my fields they welcome were,
I never welcome was to her.
        Tho' to my, &c.

If Nanny ever loſt a ſheep,
   I cheerfully did give her two:
Did not her lambs in ſafety ſleep
   Within my folds in froſt and ſnow?
Have they not there from cold been free?
But Nanny ſtill is cold to me.
       Have they not, &c.

Whene'er I climb'd our orchard trees,
   The ripeſt fruit was kept for Nan;
Oh how thoſe hands that drown'd her bees
   Were ſtung! I'll ne'er forget the pain:
Sweet were the combs as ſweet could be,
But Nanny ne'er look'd ſweet on me.
      Sweet were, &c.

If Nanny to the well did come,
   'Twas I that did her pitchers fill;
Full as they were I brought them home,
   Her corn I carry'd to the mill:
My back did bear her ſacks, but ſhe
Would never bear the ſight of me.
      My back did bear, &c.

Muſt Robin always Nanny woo?
   And Nanny ſtill on Robin frown?
Alas! poor wretch! what ſhall I do,
   If Nanny does not love me ſoon?
If no relief to me ſhe'll bring,
I'll hang me in her apron ſtring.
      If no relief, &c.

SONG C.

SALLY IN OUR ALLEY.

Of all the girls that are so

smart, There's none like pret - - ty Sal - - - ly,

She is the dar - - ling of my heart,

And she lives in our - - - - - al - - - ley;

There's ne'er a la - - dy in the land That's

half so sweet as Sal - - - ly,   For she's the

darling   of   my   heart, And she lives   in

our   al - - - ley,

Her father he makes cabbage nets
    For those that want to buy 'em,
Her mother she makes laces long,
    And thro' the streets does cry 'em :
But sure such folks cou'd ne'er beget
    So sweet a girl as Sally,
She is the darling of my heart,
    And she lives in our alley.

When she is by I leave my work,
    I love her so sincerely,
My master comes like any Turk,
    And bangs me most severely :
But let him bang his belly full,
    I'll bear it all for Sally.

For she's the darling of my soul,
  And she lives in our alley.

Of all the days into the week,
  I dearly love but one day,
And that's the day that comes between
  A Saturday and Monday;
For then I'm dreſt in all my beſt,
  To walk abroad with Sally,
For she's the darling of my soul,
  And she lives in our alley.

My maſter carries me to church,
  Where often I am blamed,
Becauſe I leave him in the lurch,
  As ſoon as text is named.
I leave the church in ſermon time,
  And ſlink away to Sally,
For she's the darling of my soul,
  And she lives in our alley.

My maſter, and the neighbours all,
  Make game of me and Sally,
Wer't not for her, I'd better be
  A ſlave and row a galley;
For when my ſeven long years are out,
  Why then I'll marry Sally,
Then we'll wed—and then we'll bed,
  But not into our alley.

SONG CI.

Tune—*Johnny's Grey Breeks.*

Now smiling spring a --- gain appears, With

all the beau -- ties of her train, Love

foon of her ar --- riv -- al hears, And flies

to wound the gentle swain. How gay does

nature now appear, The lambkins frisking

o'er the plain, Sweet feather'd song-sters now

we hear, While Jenny seeks her gen-tle

swain. How gay does nature now appear, The

lambkins frisking o'er the plain, Sweet fea-

ther'd songsters now we hear, While Jenny

seeks her gentle swain.

Ye nymphs, O! lead me to the grove,
    Thro' which your ftreams in filence mourn
There with my Johnny let me rove,
    'Till once his fleecy flock return:
Young Johnny is my loving fwain,
    He fweetly pipes along the mead,
So foon's the lambkins hear his ftrain,
    With eager fteps return in fpeed.

The flocks, now all in fportive play,
    Come frifking round the piping fwain,
Then, fearful of too long delay,
    Run bleating to their dams again:
Within the frefh green myrtle grove,
    The feather'd choir in rapture fing,
And fweetly warble forth their love,
    To welcome the returning fpring.

SONG CII.

EMMA.

To the foregoing Tune.

CREATION fmiles on ilka fide,
    In lively green the fields appear,
While cuckoos publifh far and wide,
    That fummer's florid beauty's near.
And fhall I peerlefs Emma find
    Still blufhing fweet with native charms?
And will the faireft o' her kind
    Confent to blefs my langing arms?

Again we tryſt, and punctual meet,
   Far, far beyond yon riſing hill,
Where black birds ſing and lambkins bleat,
   In concert with the gurgling rill.
Nae miſer's wealth, nae ſtateſmen's fame,
   Nae toper's joy envied I ſee,
While room within her breaſt I claim,
   That's wealth, and fame, and joy to me.

With counterfeited ſlee deſign,
   Equipt the angler, aft I gang,
Yet flee, or bait, or art of mine,
   The ſpeckled trouts but ſeldom wrang.
Enjoy your wanton random ſpouts,
   Ye harmleſs tenants of the ſtream,
While I enjoy what better ſuits
   A thrilling heart—my love's eſteem.

Where ſcented woodbines form a ſhade,
   And birks their neighbour birks embrace,
I'll kiſs the dear enticing maid,
   While ſweeteſt bluſhes paint her face.
May friendſhip bleeze with Hymen's flame,
   A doubly-tender tye to caſt,
And time row round ilk day the ſame,
   The future happy as the paſt.

Ye woodland ſangſters join with me,
   Ye dimpling ſtreams that curling glide,
Ye winds that ſough thro' ilka tree,
   Hail, Emma—Hail my charming bride.
Then Fortune at thy ſhrine I'll bow,
   Indulgent hear my anxious prayer;
 " A frugal competence allow,
   " Nor free, nor deep haraſs'd with care."

SONG CIII.

BANKS OF THE SHANNON.

In summer when the leaves were green,

And blos-soms deck'd each tree, Young

Teddy then declar'd his love, His artless

love to me: On Shannon's flow'ry banks

we sat, And there he told his tale: "Oh

Pat - ty, soft - est of thy sex, Oh let fond

love prevail; Ah, well - a - day, You see me

pine in for - row and de - - - fpair, Yet

heed me not, then let me die, And end my

grief and care."—"Ah no, dear youth, I foft-

ly faid, Such love demands my thanks:

K k

And here I vow e - -ter - nal truth on

Shannon's   flow'ry   banks.

And then we vow'd eternal truth
On Shannon's flow'ry banks,
And then we gather'd fweeteft flowers,
And play'd fuch artlefs pranks:
But, woe is me, the prefs-gang came,
And forc'd my Ned away,
Juft when we nam'd next morning fair,
To be our wedding day.

My love, he cry'd, they force me hence,
But ftill my heart is thine,
All peace be yours, my gentle Pat,
While war and toil is mine.
With riches I'll return to thee,
I fobb'd out words of thanks,
And then we vow'd eternal truth,
On Shannon's flow'ry banks.

And then we vow'd eternal truth,
On Shannon's flow'ry banks,
And then I faw him fail away,
And join the hoftile ranks.

From morn to eve, for twelve dull months,
　His abſence ſad I mourn'd,
The peace was made, the ſhip came back,
　But Teddy ne'er return'd.

His beauteous face and manly form
　Has won a nobler fair;
My Teddy's falſe, and I, forlorn,
　Muſt die in ſad deſpair.
Ye gentle maidens, ſee me laid,
　While you ſtand round in ranks,
And plant a willow o'er my head,
　On Shannon's flow'ry banks.

SONG CIV.

AT SETTING DAY AND RISING MORN.

Tune—*Mill, Mill, O.*

Slow.

At set-ting day, and ri--sing morn,

Wi' foul that still shall love thee,

I'll afk of heav'n thy fafe return,

Wi' a' that can im------prove

thee. I'll vi---fit aft the bir--ken

bufh, Where fuft thou kind---ly tald me

Sweet tales of love, and hid my blufh, Whilft

round thou didft en - - - - - - fold   me.

To a' our haunts I will repair,
    By greenwood fhaw or fountain;
Or where the fimmer day I'd fhare
    Wi' thee upon yon mountain:
There will I tell the trees and flow'rs,
    From thoughts unfeign'd and tender,
By vows you're mine, by love is yours
    A heart which cannot wander.

SONG CV.

OH NANNY, WILT THOU GANG WI' ME?

Oh Nan - ny, wilt thou gang wi' me,

Nor figh to leave the flaunting town? Can

fil - - ent glens have charms for thee, The

low - - - ly cote and ruf - fet gown?

No longer drefs'd in filk - en fheen, No

longer   deck'd   with   jew - els   rare,   Say,

can'ft   thon   quit   the   bu - fy   fcene,   Where

thou   art   fair - - - eft   of   the   fair.

O Nanny, when thou'rt far awa,
　　Wilt thou not caft a wifh behind?
Say, can'ft thou face the flaky fnaw,
　　Nor fhrink before the warping wind?
O can that faft and gentleft mien
　　Severeft hardfhips learn to bear?
Nor fad, regret each courtly fcene,
　　Where thou wert faireft of the fair?

O Nanny, can'ft thou love fo true,
　　Thro' perils keen wi' me to gae,
Or when thy fwain mifhap fhall rue,
　　To fhare with him the pang of wae?
And when invading pains befal,
　　Wilt thou affume the nurfe's care,
Nor, wifhful, thofe gay fcenes recal,
　　Where thou wert faireft of the fair?

And when, at laſt, thy love ſhall die,
    Wilt thou receive his parting breath?
Wilt thou reprefs each ſtruggling ſigh,
    And cheer with ſmiles the bed of death?
And wilt thou, o'er his much lov'd clay,
    Strew flowers, and drop the tender tear,
Nor then regret thoſe ſcenes ſo gay,
    Where thou wert faireſt of the fair?

SONG CVI.

THE WAWKING OF THE FAULD

Andante.

My Peg - gy is a young thing, Juſt enter'd

in her teens, Fair as the day, and ſweet as

May, Fair as the day, and always gay; My

Peg - gy is a young thing, And I'm not

ve - ry auld, Yet wiel I like to meet her at

L l

The wawking of the fauld. My Peg-gy

fpeaks fae fweetly, Whene'er we meet alane, I

with. nae mair to lay my care, I wifh nae

mair of a' that's rare; My Peggy fpeaks fae

fweet-ly, To a' the lave I'm cauld; But

She gars a' my fpirits glow at wawking

of the fauld.

My Peggy fmiles fae kindly,
  Whene'er I whifper love,
That I look down on a' the town,
That I look down upon a crown ;
  My Peggy fmiles fae kindly,
    It makes me blyth and bauld,
  And naething gi'es me fic delight
    As wawking of the fauld.

My Peggy fings fae faftly,
  When on my pipe I play :
By a' the reft it is confeft,
By a' the reft that fhe fings beft :
  My Peggy fings fae faftly,
    And in her fangs are tald,
  Wi' innocence, the wale of fenfe,
    At wawking of the fauld.

SONG CVII.

CUMBERNAULD HOUSE.

Slow.

Where wind - - - ing Forth a - - - dorns

the vale, Fond Stre - phon, once a

fhep - herd gay, Did to the rocks his

lot be - wail, And thus ad - - dreft his

plaintive lay: O   Julia, more than

lil - - - - ly fair, More blooming than the

op'-ning rofe, How can thy breaft re-

lent-lefs wear A heart more cold than

Winter's fnows.

Yet nipping Winter's keeneft reign,
    But for a fhort-liv'd fpace prevails;
Spring time returns, and cheers each fwain,
    Seented with Flora's fragrant gales.
Come, Julia, come, thy love obey,
    Thou miftrefs of angelic charms,
Come fmiling like the morn of May,
    And centre in thy Strephon's arms.

Elſe, haunted by the fiend Deſpair,
　He'll court ſome ſolitary grove,
Where mortal foot did ne'er repair,
　But ſwains oppreſs'd with hapleſs love.
From the once-pleaſing rural throng
　Remov'd, he'll bend his lonely way,
Where Philomela's mournful ſong
　Shall join his melancholy lay.

SONG CVIII.

To the foregoing Tune.

FROM anxious zeal and factious ſtrife,
And all th'uneaſy cares of life,
From beauty, ſtill to merit blind,
And ſtill to fools and coxcombs kind;
To where the woods, in brighteſt green,
Like riſing theatres are ſeen,
Where gently murm'ring runs the rill,
And draws freſh ſtreams from ev'ry hill:

Where Philomel, in mournful ſtrains,
Like me, of hopeleſs love complains;
Retir'd I paſs the livelong day,
And idly trifle life away:

My lyre to tender accents ftrung,
I tell each flight, each fcorn and wrong,
Then reafon to my aid I call,
Review paft fcenes, and fcorn them all,

Superior thoughts my mind engage,　·
Allur'd by Newton's tempting page,
Through new-found worlds I wing my flight,
And trace the glorious fource of light:
But fhould Clarinda there appear,
With all her charms of fhape and air,
How frail my fixt refolves would prove!
Again I'd yield, again I'd love!

SONG CIX.

THE LAKE OF KILLARNEY.

Allegretto.

On the Lake of   Kil - - lar - - ney   I

firſt ſaw the lad, Who with ſong and with

bagpipe   could make my heart glad, On the

Lake of Killar - ney I firſt ſaw the lad, Who

with song and with bagpipe cou'd make my

heart glad: And his hair was so red, and his

eyes were so bright, Oh they shone like the

stars in a cold frost-ty night, So tall and

so straight my dear Paddy was seen, Oh he

look'd like the fairies that dance on the green.

M m

Andantino.

On the, &c. All the girls of Killar - ney wore

green willow tree, When firft my dear Patrick

fung love tales to me, Oh he fung and he

danc'd, and he won my fond heart, And to

fave his dear life, with my own I wou'd part.

D. C.

On the, &c.

SONG CX.

Tune—*Broom of Cowden-Knows.*

See page 142.

WHEN fummer comes, the fwains on Tweed
    Sing their fuccefsful loves,
Around the ewes and lambkins feed,
    And mufic fills the groves.

But my lov'd fong is then the broom,
    So fair on Cowden-knows;
For fure fo fweet, fo foft a bloom
    Elfewhere there never grows.

There Colin tun'd his oaten reed,
    And won my yielding heart;
No fhepherd e'er that dwelt on Tweed
    Could play with half fuch art.

He fung of Tay, of Forth, and Clyde,
    The hills and dales all round,
Of Leader-haughs, and Leader-fide;
    Oh! how I blefs'd the found!

Yet more delightful is the broom
    So fair on Cowden-knows;
For fure fo frefh, fo bright a bloom
    Elfewhere there never grows.

Not Tiviot braes, fo green and gay,
    May with this broom compare,
Not Yarrow banks in flow'ry May,
    Nor the bufh aboon Traquair.

More pleasing far are Cowden-knows,
   My peaceful happy home,
Where I was wont to milk my ewes
   At e'en among the broom.

Ye powers that haunt the woods and plains,
   Where Tweed with Tiviot flows,
Convey me to the best of swains,
   And my lov'd Cowden-knows.

SONG CXI.

THE ADIEU.

Amoroso.

A - - dieu, ye streams that smooth - - ly

flow, Ye ver - - nal airs that soft - - - - - ly

blow, Ye plains by bloom - ing Spring

ar - ray'd, Ye birds that war - ble through

the glade, Ye birds that war - - - ble

thro' the glade, Un - hurt from you my

foul could fly, Nor drop one tear,

nor heave one figh, But forc'd from

Ce - - - - lia's fmiles to part, All

joy de - - - ferts my droop - - - - ing

heart, All 'joy de - - ferts my

droop - - ing heart.

O fairer than the rofy morn,
When flow'rs the dewy fields adorn,
Unfully'd as the genial ray,
That warms the gentle breeze of May;
Thy charms divinely fweet appear,
And add new fplendor to the year,
Improve the day with frefh delight,
And gild with joy the dreary night.

FINIS.

www.ingramcontent.com/pod-product-compliance
Lightning Source LLC
Chambersburg PA
CBHW030348270326
41926CB00009B/1012